JUMPING OVER LIFE HURDLES
AND STAYING IN THE RACE

LORENZO P. LEWIS

Dedication

I dedicate this book to Phyllis and Jacky Johnson, thank you for giving me life and evermore the tender-loving care in the early years when you were able to. To my Aunt Daisy and Uncle T. Royal life wouldn't be what it was if it wasn't for your patience, fortitude and strength in the early years of my childhood. I was lost, hurt and trying to find my way, thank you for never giving up. I will always adore you both for that. To my Daughter Sareya, you have huge shoes to fill. I will give you love and fulfillment as your father every day I can. You are destined for greatness. Your seat will be waiting for you in the boardroom and a legacy to walk in forever.

To every Black Man and Sister in America don't shy away from telling your truth walk bold, with your chest high and regardless of what the world tells us, we are better we are genius we are everything they say we are not and couldn't be. Tell your story because if you don't someone else will!

iv

Table of Contents

Chapter 1
The First Leg

Newark, New Jersey was in the midst of turning into something great, a place of city life, urban transportation, and busy traffic stretching across the nightlife towards Atlantic City. The climate was entrepreneurs, businessmen, corporate players and hustlers. This was the best fit for what was brewing inside of Hudson County Hospital.

Sporty, better known as Jacky Ray Johnson, was a southern boy who was on a mission to build a countryman's dream of riches. My mother, Phyllis Lewis was a free spirit with a dream of taking a different path. They were both travelers and focused on the grind of hustling for the next idea or dream.

In the womb my mother passed on those powerful traveling genes and a hardworking spirit that would fuel a man, a KING, to confront and share his past with other men who need to confront their own. I was a child born ready to share, travel, and speak. On May 8, 1988,

Lorenzo Pierre Lewis was born ready to storm a world that was waiting to swallow him up. My world would be cloaked in night darkness, dominated by struggle, and swung with the wind of hesitation, but all this would produce a divine, but modest black man, in the space we call society.

I was born in bondage; not the physical bondage of the institutional walls my mother was serving time in, as required by the courts and jurisdiction of New Jersey, but the inescapable bondage of a child whose parent is detained by the American justice system.

Initially, my father was the caregiver while my mom was being held on the small sentence. My arrival forced him to take a break from the hustle, but he was thankful for his offspring. He was also anxious for my mom to join him. But, the draw of the open road and the hustle was too much. A friend of my mother's eventually took me in. She loved having me and begged my mother to keep me. While I am grateful for her early care and desire to raise and love me, my aunt wanted a permanent and legal resolution to my care. My parents' limited opportunities and lack of personal and social growth made my natural parents an unstable at best. Though my mom's friend may have been a great mother, my family wanted me to stay family. Arkansas, where my Aunt and Uncle lived, became HOME.

This was the game changer. My Aunt and Uncle, Daisy and Tee Lee had a full plate, but stepped-in and took full responsibility for me, her brother's child. They knew the arrangement would provide stability and be rich in growth for me, their nephew. So, at four months old, I became a guest and eventually a resident in the house. I was surrounded by a family: four kids, a husband and wife, and of course me—the newborn.

My youth was spent hearing the exploits of their traveling lifestyle. They ran from coast to coast, living the street life, working toward their vision of success. Their determination and risk taking was reflected in both my youthful exploits and the difficulties I conquered.

Junk Miles

Growing up without my biological mother and father was often a topic of conversation in social settings. In most of my conversations, I remember being the odd kid out who didn't want to say why my biological parents weren't in the picture.

Once, we had mother and father show and tell at school, and all the kids were excited and ready to show their parents off. My aunt and uncle were there, ready to talk, but despite being grateful for their presence, I was torn apart by the thought that my "real" parents wouldn't be there. More than that, I was mostly bothered by not knowing what my parents did for a living. When it came to writing down their occupations during the class activity, I was at a loss. I had to leave it blank. The other kids made fun of me for not knowing my parents' occupations. I was a 4th grader and couldn't even tell you what they actually did or, the last time I spoke to them.

My Aunt Daisy always did a great job letting me see my siblings and keep in touch with distant family. At the time, my mother lived in Mobile, Alabama and my father continued to travel. By the time was in the middle of elementary school, my father's health had started to get worse. Sporty was a rolling stone, moving from state to state, taking the east coast by storm, and even moving to California. But, during that cold December in Memphis, Tennessee, none of us had any idea that the days of Sporty were coming to an abrupt finish.

My lack of knowledge and resources to cope with this loss led me to create brick by brick, an emotional wall, and led to feelings that my biological parents were not necessary in my life. I ruthlessly suppressed my feelings related to my parents and the injustice of being told to not be angry and hateful towards my situation. I became an almost ten-year-old black boy with unexplainable anxiety in the classroom and around peers, and I was lost in wondering if life would always be this way. The narrative I created was that either I wasn't good enough to have my parents or they were not concerned enough. My narrative is the same story that many young black and brown boys face in America.

Lactic Acid

Grade school was where I discovered that my story would tangibly be judged, and I would be seen as a positive or negative, completely dependent on who was judging. The most positive judgments came from people who knew me best: my family.

As an adult, it has been a sweet blessing to realize how much I gained in having siblings and the structure of family, especially after being separated at birth from my biological siblings.

While I lived in Arkansas, I had a brother in Memphis and a sister in Mobile. Pops also had three other boys, who were part of the crew. But we all lived apart, raised by other family members. Even in the midst of such love and acceptance, where I was treated no differently than my cousins, that I considered to be brothers and sisters, I saw myself as the outsider. Outside my family, an early memory I have of being seen in a positive light was the beginning of kindergarten. Sweet Ms. Everson was probably one of the best teachers I had in all my school experience. She was kind and treated me as another child with seeds of potential.

Unfortunately, not every teacher was Ms. Everson. Public schools seemed to be a place where authority figures were more likely to see me, and my story, in a negative light. This was the start of misunderstandings and small behavior issues, which would become bigger behavior and social issues.

By the start of third grade I had taken to being the class clown in a bid for attention. With a lack of guidance and no idea of how or where to focus my talent and strengths, my time and energy was spent being disruptive. In a place where fitting-in and towing the line is rewarded, the cycle of attention seeking and consequences would snowball into oppression, racism, and an ADHD diagnosis. My teacher was white, and whether purposeful or not, simply did not listen to or engage with me. I was pre-diagnosed and referred to as a student who could not learn and was not competent in academics among my peers. I remember, bright as day, my third-grade teacher stating that I would not be able to keep up and I would not make it past her class. Thus, started the cultural narrative of: "You won't be anything in life." As an eight-year-old African American male, this was only the beginning of my traumatic experience in public schools.

The lack of engagement with the adults in secondary education led to my behavior problems becoming worse. In class, I continued to interrupt teachers, laugh at and disrespect teachers, and was consumed with using curse words. I was grieving the loss of my parents in my everyday life and my teachers did not understand how to work with my trauma induced behavior issues. All this led to low test scores and poor performance.

A teacher recommended test for Special Education. I was also tested for ADHD and psychological issues. The tests came back normal, of course, and I was separated and treated differently than every student in my classroom for the remainder of the semester. Separating me from my peers led to more problems and everything came to a head the next term when the school guidance counselor requested that I be sent to an intervention program/camp for disturbed and struggling boys in the public-school setting. Home was still a refuse where I felt understood, and with camp on the horizon, I knew change was coming, but I had no idea what the change would be so final.

"Negative Splits"

December 14, 1997 started with a cold morning. I remember it was quite early and the house was at rest. There was Christmas music playing in the background because this close to Christmas, the Lees played Christmas music throughout the night. The sound of Christmas music filling every room made the season stand out and I looked forward to it every year. On that typical morning, the phone rang several times, but in my mind, it seemed to go on forever and a wrenching feeling settled in my stomach. Even though my father's death was unexpected, as the phone rang, I felt sick because something inside me knew that news that could never be taken back was on the other end of the phone. A hysterical scream, both scary and nerve wracking, came from the other room.

The news my father was pronounced dead during the early morning hours seemed like a dream. My aunt in shock and my uncle held her as she grappled with the intense shock of the news. I was an eight-year-old boy who had few memories of my dad, but I was still hurt and confused. The loss of my biological father, who I had not known well enough to look up to, left me dependent on the only father I could look up to, my uncle. Even in the midst of comforting his wife, my Uncle Tee, a man who carried himself with the integrity, proved himself ROYAL when he hugged and comforted me. The entire household was in disbelief.

The more I think about it, I am unsure if I realized how bad the cancer was. As an eight-year-old kid, I did not understand terminal illness and the possibility of death. Yet, I had to live it. The funeral was disheartening and probably one of the worst settings I could ever imagine. The funeral was all sadness, with hysterical screams of family members, sorrowful singing from the choir, and personal testimonies of his importance in people's lives. It was sorrow heaped on sorrow, heard and seen by a boy who had simply not known that man.

I hated funerals at this point; I recognized them as a horrific dream that never ended, I remember going through counseling shortly after the burial of my father. This was when actual counselors were present in the public schools. Ms. Rice was the "Mother" of the school. She was comforting, and made sure us little black boys had a positive woman role model to speak to, and share our joys and shortcomings with. As you might imagine, my father's death had not improved my behavior issues. I was a menace in the classroom and was a distraction to my peers. I didn't care about or for anyone. I was confused about how I, as a little black boy, with a dead father and an absent mother could have or give the same affection as everyone else. I wondered about if I'd still be able to see my brothers and sisters. My reality was harsh and I had so few answers to my many questions that I reacted in ways I thought would get me answers. The only answer that behavior got me was a recommendation that I be put in another school setting.

Joseph Pfeifer Camp was a camp for adolescents to gain social structure and implement positive behaviors. I'm still unsure if everyone there attended as a consequence of misconduct at school, or if there were other reasons students were enrolled. I recall being in tears as my aunt dropped off for the first day. At almost nine years old, transitioning to living away from home for three months, with only weekend passes, was life altering. Surprisingly, it turned out to be a pleasant experience.

The campers were split between seven or eight cabins. We went to school for six to seven hours a day, sang songs, and walked military style coming and going around the facility. We dressed alike, learned value of respect, and how to be protective of your brother. I also learned what it was like to have an adult, outside of my family, care about me and my future.

Mr. Jesse was my first real protector and friend He was a good listener when I needed someone to talk to about the loss of my father. He let me stay up later than the other camps to talk about how I felt. He faces me time to process my emotions when I was angry. He recognized that I needed the time to process when I acted out and administered camp consequences with grace. After losing my father and moving away to Camp Pfeiffer, Mr. Jesse's sincere desire to help me and willingness to comfort me was an anchor.

The weekends home was awesome, but very short, and before I knew it, I had completed the camp curriculum and was approved to graduate. I headed back to fourth grade with intentions to be a better student and respect and honor others. I knew I'd need to be diligent in applying all I had learned in my time at Camp Pfeifer. This need to be diligent in maintaining structure, and continually working to respect and honor others, has proved a lifetime journey. I also learned that while structure made space for change, helpful, guidance in the midst of struggle is even more necessary. Going into a foreign environment and meeting new people to provide the therapy I needed was exactly what I needed.

My aunt and her family took a chance on Camp Pfeiffer because they knew I needed more help than they could give. They didn't fully understand childhood trauma, so they found professionals who did. That leap of faith changed my life. Chances make champions, and my aunt and uncle are just that; they championed my journey and never led me astray. The power of support and prayer is critical.

In Matthew 21:22, it says, "And whatever you ask in prayer, you will receive, if you have faith." By having a praying aunt that wanted peace and healing for a hurting child that experienced a devastating loss, I was supported, even when I didn't know it. Our faith was the only thing that got us through. Praying for me when I couldn't pray for myself. Loving me with no strings attached. I was on course to be a better me.

Cool Down

During life you will encounter many issues, just like I did. You will lose people you love. You will be a part of traumatic experiences that will literally make you want to give up. You will be told you are not good enough. You will be labeled, and most of all, you will see everything that life has to show you. But that vision will not unfold easily or happily, but tinted with the cruelty of dreams seemingly out of reach.

How was I able to deal with the story leading to my my birthright? What person would want to know that they were born in a prison? Or better yet, to parents both incarcerated. I can tell you what, no one will be prepared to tell that story. And to this day, I am still surprised to find myself actually telling this story, again; everyone in the room's mouth will drop and souls are shaking. But there are practical ways you can process through trauma like this and can help anyone who is dealing with hard life circumstances they have no control over.

Practice Gratitude…

Thank your higher source, whether that's GOD or a different higher source. Just sit in pure Gratitude about how things came together to get you here on Earth. Sometimes this is easier said than done; I can attest that being thankful for anything you totally didn't have control over will be difficult. Maybe you are not battling that your story didn't start off in a prison, but started off in abuse, neglect, or separation from your parents or caregivers. There is hurt and burden behind any situation that is not the norm. I define the norm as living with both parents, siblings living in the same house, e.g. But knowing that you are able to endure the strength and pressure that got you to this point will be important for your overall success. There was a time that I didn't want to acknowledge GOD (or another higher source), who loved me so much, would give me the burden of saying my story started in a prison. I earned my stripes early, and you will too. Your wings will prepare you to fight the battles you will face later in life.

You will need SUPPORT…

Losing my biological father, and not living with my parents, truly gave me my inner strength. Honestly, once you go through significant hurt you strengthen your emotional muscles for the next fight you will face. Life's hurdles are tough, but they are doable, and you can STAY IN THE RACE By embracing your pain instead of pushing it away. The next time you face another hurdle much different.

That being said, because I was so young when I lost my father that I was unequipped emotionally and lacked the necessary coping skills. When this happens you automatically feel unequipped. What did help me was having support. My aunt and uncle did a really good job of comforting me and supporting my needs immediately after my father died. But they didn't talk about it as much in the months or years after he passed. Not unless it was my father's birthday or holiday moments. And the burden of support shouldn't just be on one or two people, so find your VILLAGE, or BUILD YOUR VILLAGE. Either way, get the support you will need to endure the heartache tragedy. Building the village means go and find the people that will support you—I would never have guessed that many of the people who have walked me through my tragedy are not directly related to me.Building your support team will help you to endure the race even longer and, ultimately, not give up.

Create a Plan, And Don't Give Up…

When I look back, ending up in Joseph Pfeifer Camp, which is described as an alternative classroom and summer camp, quickly following the loss of my father and being singled out, as many children of color are, by a white teacher in an institution rife with systemic racism, is still one of the craziest moments I've ever had. What I had to realize is that once you find yourself in a pressed place, not knowing how to move forward, then is the time to think about creating a plan against not giving up completely. In most cases people are pushed to give up, especially when things in life snowball back-to-back. I can remember after leaving Pfeifer Camp, immediately getting home, asking my aunt and uncle what could I do to go back to school and be better than before I left.

Even as a young man, I quickly realized that I wanted to be in a much better situation where I had control—whether that was receiving support from a better teacher or having better friends. Although I didn't have a specific plan, I asked to be put on a better track to move forward. The intuition inside of us speaks to how we need to move forward. If that small voice in your spirit is telling you to push forward, that means you need to GO forward and never quit! We all have some type of limitation impacts our our journey, but being clear about your plan to keep going is key for your success and completion.

Chapter 2
Coach, Put Me in The Game

Time passed and I barely made it out of elementary school. While I learned a lot about myself and made some changes at Camp Pfeiffer, breaking habits and facing loss takes time and persistence. Unsurprisingly, I left grade school with a less than stellar reputation, but my aunt, a strong fighter, continued to push and remind the middle school faculty that I was a young man dealing with the loss his father, and separation of siblings. Aunt Daisy was always my biggest fan; she prayed harder for me than any other mother I know. Little did I know, that despite a good beginning in middle school, I would need those prayers.

The 7th grade was light to the darkness of elementary school. There were new friends, new ways to mingle, and of course, meeting new girls; by this time, I realized I was the chubby boy, but it didn't stop me from trying. I was sure girls liked a guy who wasn't like everyone else, and I had been different down to a science.

My patient uncle spent more than he imagined buying more school clothes and shoes to support my quest to impress the girls at school. I was twelve years old and girl crazy. My aunt and uncle tried to get me interested in other things, but you couldn't tell me no different. My transition to junior high that year was full of optimism. I was ready to find a social circle, something to be a part of, a unique way to stand out. My life was cliques and groups: rap groups, the football and basketball players, and the thugs and skippers who missed class to get high in the bathroom (It was always during fifth period after lunch, because security had already finished their sweep and never came to the back hall to check for loose students). There was plenty of trees smoked in that bathroom, money gambled, and sex had. We were trying to live our lives like a 50 Cent song.

Imagine twelve to fifteen-year-olds indulging in this behavior. Led by the power of rap music, society had us brainwashed and we were determined to be just like the music we listened to and things we saw on TV. I did not keep up with schoolwork that year; I had a total blast the entire seventh grade. It was not an issue of my ability to learn, I was at level for reading and was as academically as gifted as the next kid; I just would not focus. I learned the hard way. I failed the seventh grade. It was devastating.

That summer I begged my aunt to switch schools. She was determined that I would not switch, and I would get a taste of my own medicine. All those evenings of coming home lying about having no homework had caught up. Dread made me feel sick and not up for the embarrassment of facing my peers, that summer I hid the notice the school sent in the mail, the notice stamped "RETAINED." I knew it was true, but I was in denial, I had wrongly assumed my aunt would somehow get me into eighth grade. I could not believe that I was going to have to do the whole year over. Instead of a first day of eighth grade, I had a second first day of seventh grade.

The first day of retained seventh grade, I was sitting in my first class and for some reason the class was happening on the cafeteria stage, behind the stage curtains Of course, first days of class are introductions, checklists, and rules. I was so over it, and trying to avoid catching the attention of my class.

Let's be real, I didn't exactly blend in; I even looked older and bigger. It was horrible, and it was about to get worse. I could hear a bunch of other kids walk in the cafeteria, so I guessed lunch was starting. Meanwhile, the teacher kept saying that the room was hot and wanted to get some air. I knew what she wanted. She wanted that curtain to roll back. Regardless of the consequences, I was about to RUN for it. I tried to rationalize wanting to run with the thought, "I can't get put out of school it's just the first day of school." All the while I was remembering my aunt telling me she wasn't having it this year. So, I stayed. The curtains rolled back. I saw all my classmates from the year before and I was sure the entire cafeteria was laughing at me. I tried to cover my head, like that would effectively hide me.

The reaction was the exact opposite of what I hoped for. Suddenly, I didn't blend in, I had drawn attention to myself, and the other students caught on and started asking questions. While this was not great in the moment, I was forced to be honest about failing, and the reasons why I failed. Ultimately, it made me stronger and challenged me to be better in all aspects of my life.

Repeating the seventh grade also gave me an edge when it came to middle school basketball tryouts. I grew up a basketball fan, not a fan of any particular team, but a fan of the game. I could handle that rock. I was determined to make it PRO. My inspiration was the brother of my heart and cousin of my blood, Terrance Lee. Blood couldn't have made us any closer.

Tale, as he was called, was a phenomenon in the great state of Arkansas. T.Lee, a 97' graduate of Robinson High School, was an amazing basketball player. His high school sports career was covered in newspaper article after article and on media stations left and right. T.Lee was the next great thing, and all I wanted was to follow in his footsteps. I spent many days going to the community center and gyms, and playing on outside courts and in summer league games at Dunbar Community Center. My hard work and having a role model to look up to paid off when I tried out for the eighth-grade basketball team and made it!

As the chubby kid, Coach stayed on me about my weight, but I wasn't interested. I had enough game to match anyone on the team, but because of not getting off the weight I couldn't keep up with the other players. I stayed in the post, and my wide frame kept the opposing defender off me. But I was shorter than 5'10", so there wasn't much hope for being the center. I practiced hard that whole summer before ninth grade, determined to make the basketball team. When the time for high school tryouts came, I would make the team, and it was a monumental part of my teenage life.

I was also recruited heavily for football because the football coaches saw a bigger kid with quick feet, who had good hand to eye coordination; which is a plus as a high school offensive or defensive lineman with a large frame. It turned out not to be the best fit for me, but I gave it a fair try. In the end, all I cared for was basketball. Being an urban black boy from the south you were rapping, playing sports, or selling dope. It was a simple science, and I wanted to see how far I could get with the inspirations of the neighborhood superstars I had watched growing up. Those hoop dreams didn't last forever, but when they failed, I was already working on the next thing.

During my hoop dreams my uncle inspired me to work. He never forced me because I wanted my own money and had the work ethic to get it. I worked hard for my earliest earnings: I remember 100-degree summers of cutting yards, and chilly autumn falls raking leaves at his rental houses. That work helped me cultivate a real go-getter spirit. I still think my work ethic is one of the best attributes I could have learned. That stands firm today, a man must work to eat.

Middle school also meant long bus rides to school. I was up by six in the morning and on the bus by half past six. Mom wasn't playing about that bus ride, either. Missing the bus was not a part of any answer. In middle school, I was still being bussed out of the city into a rural area, about a thirty- or forty-minute drive. The long bus rides taught me a lot. I thought a lot and listened to some of the best gangster rap music. This was the era of the late 2pac, three 6 mafia, and beginning T.I. I built long lasting connections with the other kids on the bus because when you have a bunch of city youth going to school in rural of area, it bonds you. My days were framed with super long rides, loud ear phones, cell phones, and beepers. Back in the day, we all snuck the Motorola's to school.

While working on my uncle's rental properties gave me a taste of work, my first real job came at sixteen. My aunt and uncle knew that I was a hustler by spirit. I was ambitious and wanted to work, so it didn't take long. Wendy's gave me a chance. While it didn't pay much, it was definitely a wise time investment; every young black man needs to know the value of a hard-working dollar, and I learned accuracy, speaking skills, accountability and determination.

Without realizing it, this job molded me for the next decades of working I endured. Being a grill man taught me integrity and to appreciate the small things in life. I worked my butt off for $5.75 an hour. It was a decent enough wage to let me buy some new shoes every week. Having a sense of ownership and knowing that I had my own earnings going into a checking and savings account mattered to sixteen-year-old me I worked with men that said that this job would teach me the life best lessons, and they were right.

Rush hour in a fast food restaurant was critical because it taught me about endurance. The long hours in the freezer packaging French fries and hamburger meat in below freezing temperatures reinforced that I had to keep my eye on the prize and not give in to frustration or boredom. The accuracy needed in this task also taught me to value completion and detail work. I also gained people skills. I met diverse individuals in this setting, the good and the ugly. I met those who had no choice but to work at a fast food restaurant because they had a criminal record, those like myself who were in their the first job to open the door to the world of work, and those who capitalized off management and used the job as a stepping stone for a better life. I had every example to learn from and decide how I could make my experience or my next move. Along with the good, it was also a place where I made bad choices.

Wendy's was where I first tried marijuana. I was working a shift with a close friend and he introduced me to weed. He said, "Man this will change your life and make you feel good about yourself." What it actually felt like was floating with elevated shoes that extended me to seven feet tall. It kicked my butt. I felt sick to my stomach and dizzy. I still can't figure out how regular users loved the sensation or used it regularly. I was ridiculous for trying such things at sixteen-years-old. I wanted to fit in with the rest of the guys. Being high like everyone else was cool and the thing to do. My desire to fit in pushed me to make bad choices.

That first time I inhaled marijuana it felt as my lungs was going to shut down, I started coughing and couldn't stop. The other guys just balled and laughed at me. But, because I knew it was the cool thing to do, I continued to smoke and smoke. I was so high; I seriously thought I was going to have to check into the hospital. I was scared to go home, and it was getting late. When I got home, I acted as if I was sick and had eaten something at work that gave me food poisoning. I couldn't let my aunt and uncle know I had tried weed; they weren't going for that. If they had found out it would have ended with a beat down, I wasn't ready for.

That night felt so long as I stared at the ceiling for hours. I felt bad that I had tried weed, and I promised myself that I would not do it again. I was sure if I could get over the "highness" I would be okay. I learned some valuable lessons at 16; I also did a lot of crazy things to fit in. I wasn't always a wise young brother.

Any word to anyone raising young sixteen-year-old males, particular black males: we are intrigued with what we see, we are not hard to convince, and we want to have our cake and eat it too. Decision making and peer pressure kicks our butt. At such a young age, I did not have the wisdom to understand what the old folks would tell us about doing the right thing, being around the right people, and making good decisions. I listened, and all that was fine, but it sometimes takes trying it before young men understand the burden that it may hold.

I learned good work ethic and people skills while working at Wendy's, but also, I tried some dumb shit. When you're a youth, risk taking seems like an everyday tool to get by. Despite those choices, I would not trade my time working at Wendy's for anything. It helped me become the man I am today!

Cool Down

We all want our shot! We are ready to test the waters, get in the game, and make it happen. Sometimes jumping in the game is not the easiest, and once we jump in, we have to deal with the swim. What I learned is: ask for anything, but be careful of what you ask for; you have to deal with the result. It was not the easiest enduring these challenges as a teenager. We all do the craziest things when we are young. Most of those crazy, daring, and sometimes dangerous moments turn us into the humans we are or become. I'm convinced that if you don't take chances, you won't see the value in your process, especially in your daily life.

I want you to close your eyes and think about what you wish to become. Use this exercise to elaborately visualize who you wish to become.

Let's Practice, Close Your Eyes...

Whisper to yourself and make that perfect wish of who you want to become. Choose something real and tangible so you can actually picture yourself (driving that fancy car, seeing a bank statement full of money, holding that kind and beautiful significant other, e.g.) Now, that we are visualizing this picture of you, let's try and grab for the closest object near you. Start to REACH for your phone, table, pen, e.g. While you are reaching with your eyes, don't lose that perfect picture you have started to visualize in your head. The picture-perfect life that you are living. Don't lose sight of this while grabbing the object near you.

Things Got Good, Then Things Got Rough…

When truly wanting to live a life of happiness and purpose you will begin to bump into the things you don't expect. "Coach Put Me in The Game" Embodies the idea that when you are seeking to do better, life and decisions will present themselves. I had a job, wanted to become the best version of myself through making legal money, and not hurting anybody. Then a coworker invited me to take a hit of my first joint. I could have said no. I wanted to be cool so badly. I got trapped by inner issues when what I truly needed was to understand who I was and wanted to be. Knowing yourself and going for the best thing feeds our inner self. Once you get on the straight and narrow, will things present cause confusion? ABSOLUTELY! So, be ready, know yourself, and try to make the best decision you can.

Its Ok to Fail, It's All a Temporary Process!

You have to be convinced that your life will be grand, you can be happy, and that you will face defeat and FAILURE. We all will FAIL. It's simply how we deal with failure and how we use that strength to be better the next time failure presents itself. When you are closing your eyes and picturing yourself living your best life and winning in the game of life, things will start to happen. You will be defeated, you will be lied to, someone will turn their back on you, and, yes, you will be sick about it. Think about reaching for that object when picturing yourself living your BEST LIFE. My questions for you are: why is the time right now to disturb that moment? Can it wait? Sometimes life will have things come out of the blue and disturb you. And while you think you need to reach for them, the truth is, you are not supposed to quit. Find the quiet and pay attention to how things are present themselves.

We are stronger than what we think. When you see opposition and hurt as a process that will lead to BLESSING YOU, then you may be able to help someone else who may be struggling with a similar issue.

Remain Optimistic...

Sitting down and telling yourself, in the midst of some crazy life event, "This will come to pass," feels good right? While it may not feel good (it may feel a bit weird) remaining calm, not getting angry, and thinking positive thoughts will really help you be better instantly. This is the absolute truth: once you think better about who you will become, then you will become better. You will start to feel, think, and act better. Our feelings and energy dictate how we make decisions and actions that we take. Be mindful of how your emotional energy is put into the atmosphere; this determines a major part of how you make good or bad decisions. Be positive and always live in the LIGHT… It will be hard at first to do this, but start to practice by telling yourself nice and calm things while you are going through something difficult. (I AM THE BEST, I CAN DO ANYTHING I PUT MY MIND TO, I DO ATTRACT GREATNESS, e.g.)

By announcing these commands you will start to see the positive vibration and energy flow arise and your spirit will be in a better place. Being optimistic is a game changer in any tough situation and allows you to stay in the game much longer, while reaching your greatest potential.

Chapter 3
Swifting the 200's

When I was seventeen and getting ready to start my junior year of high school. I was ready for a different environment. I had outgrown being in the sticks and was ready to make a shift. I wanted to brace the space, to be with my peers from my summers spent in the neighborhood. I begged my aunt all summer to transfer; she hesitated, and said no several times. She was wary because she knew I was getting into all kind of social circles and saw myself as part of the hip crowd. Really, they were more than a hip crowd.

By seventeen I called myself part of a gang. The summer before the 11th grade I started to run with some guys that were actually from the hood. I came up in a pretty decent area; I would classify my upbringing as lower middle class. I never grew up without lights and always had food on the table. I had nice clothes and with no rats or roaches. I chose to link up with some guys that, unlike me, lived that struggle. Their motivation for being part of a gang was different;

they really came from the hoods. They saw it as a way to survive. I didn't. I was motivated by the power of fitting in. I never got "quoted" or jumped. I was accepted for just being a cool brother and dressing really dope, like the rest of them. I was elated at this pass, not realizing I was making one of the worst mistakes of my youth.

The Bloods I ran were made up of guys in the neighborhood and other areas that I knew. All my peers were part of this hood social structure. Everybody had a hood to rep, and I definitely didn't want to feel left out. The first day at J.A. Fair High School I was finally able ride to school with the homies and skip the long bus ride. My new school had a larger population, new girls, and new sport rivalries. I had finally gotten to the other side. I had the "Black boy in the urban school setting" I had wanted, and it was the life.

I always had something to prove and was always working to fit in. I worked crazy hours at Wendy's to have all the fly clothes and shoes that were constantly releasing. I also played football that year and attended my first real football camp. We were in a bigger conference and more games were televised. Our local media was heavy on sports culture. You might think that because I of the lessons I learned in middle school I'd keep practicing till I not only made the team, but actually played. I didn't get much game time. I was too drawn into the crowds and who was going to fight after lunch the next day. I couldn't focus in practice, so I played on the practice squad. No game time for me.

As hard as that might have been, I just wanted a jersey so on Fridays all the girls could identify me as one of the cool players in the school. High school was all about cliques and groups. I gang banged during the day, missing class with the thugs, and was at football practice by five to wear my jersey. This was not the real me and peer pressure only persuaded me to make poor judgement calls and not be authentic.

It was a Friday, and the fellas had decided to skip school for senior skip day. I had done a little skipping in my time, but had yet to skip. That day that I took a risk and it changed my life. We weren't seniors just yet, but ran with all the upperclassmen. At this point, being cool was just part of the regimen.

That morning, my friend Terrell came by to get the day started with plenty of marijuana smoke blowing out of the car and loud subwoofers rattling the trunk. This was a real southern treat, weed smoke, loud music, matching tees, and a fitted cap with the skullcap to match. With a whole day to fill we decided to head to Tiger

Fest. Tiger Fest was an event Central High School put on annually for all the students across the district. It was the only time, in our public-school setting, besides a basketball or football game, where the local urban youth gather in one place to have some fun.

As we arrived, there was havoc was in the air. A few weeks prior to this event, at a nearby high school basketball game, some other guys that were representing another "clique" had jumped my best friend. He was out numbered and they had unresolved issues that led to the violence in the first place. It was the only night I wasn't with him, and they got my brother. I was pissed beyond means and was determined to pay it forward to those guys for doing my homie like that. Tiger Fest had a reputation for being the platform that all neighborhood gangs and cliques would use to follow up on old beefs. Our whole lives were about being seen and who was the top dog. Can you imagine all those high schoolers waiting all year for one event to get even? Pitiful, but true.

We entered the gate and walked through security; we were seven homies deep. We had two pistols in the group, maybe even three. We linked up with some guys from another side of town. We were feeling the extra momentum from the crowd and an urge to exact revenge for what my homie faced a few weeks ago. We're running on nothing but animosity.

I look back and wonder, were we really going to kill the guys that jumped my friend? I remember walking through the crowd, bandannas in our pocket, dark loce shades, hair twisted, and pants sagging lower than you can imagine. All eyes were on us as we approached the crowd of students. A couple of the guys who rolled with us were throwing signs and reading our body language, people began to back up. But, before we could get to the other side of the main audience, a big FIGHT broke out. The crowd scattered and security came pepper spraying and clearing out the crowd. We were seconds from making it happen.

Ironically, the guys we were searching for had just gotten into a brawl before we even laid eyes on them, and had been taken out by security and police. The more I think on it, we were seconds from firing shots on other people. As we approached the crowd, one of the guys with us cocked the pistol and released the safety. Clearly, there was not going to be much problem solving. Those guys getting busted before we got to them was a blessing in a disguise. The lord knew we didn't need to open fire in a large crowd, possibly hitting innocent bystanders. As we exited the gates, the event was shut down and the streets were jam packed, and the west side of Little Rock turned into a block party. We were young, so making a statement was always on our mind. One of the homies pulled his pistol on a random girl for laughs, scaring the heck out of her. We hopped in a Chevy pickup; we were five guys to the truck, three of us in the back of the cab and two in the front of the truck.

By this point, I'm sure girl that had the gun pulled on her had already reported the incident to the authorities. We were busy driving fast, music up, and gang signs flying. There were a lot of students in the road enjoying the aftermath of chaos that took place, which meant lots of traffic. We came through a three-way stop, there had been a shooting and a massive fight, and we slowed down to be cautious and, of course, nosey. We sped up a bit to get through the traffic and back to the other side of town.

As we were driving, some guy pointed and yelled to the nearby police, "There they go!" The police jumped in their car and begin to move towards us. I yelled through the window to my friend driving, "Speed up! The cops are getting behind us!" He sped up even though we didn't what exactly know why they were chasing us. That turned into a high-speed chase. In a neighborhood with a fifteen mile an hour speed limit, we pushed fifty to sixty mph. We went through the residential neighborhood, turning block after block, nervous as we could be. The gun had been passed to me shortly after my friend pulled it on that young lady. As we turned down another block, the police were no more than thirty feet behind us, and I took a chance to throw the gun onto someone's yard. I didn't even think about the cameras on the police cars and witnesses viewing the chase. Eventually, we pulled over.

"Everybody HANDS UP!" said two policemen with guns pointed at us, and a car behind them. We had four cops ready to pull fire if we moved an inch. The chase had only been five minutes or less, but felt like 20 minutes. We all listened to the police and stayed put. One officer approached slowly, stating, "If anyone moves, I'm firing one of you dead."

The whole thing was a traumatic experience. For the second time in my life, I had guns pulled on me. The first time was as a young man of no more than eight years old, in the country, visiting family, when a robbery took place. Unlike that day, I was the focus not of a wrongdoer's gun, but the police officers' guns. I had been raised to have respect for law enforcement, and this played back in my head. I wasn't that innocent little boy, but actually the one committing a crime.

Everyone was removed from the truck one-by-one, to lie on the ground. By this time, several police cars pulled up. Questioning took place; the police asked every one of us what we were thinking. They thought we must be the thugs who opened fire earlier that day. We all replied, at once, "NO officer it was not us."

The police replied, "Shut the hell up." They did realize I was the one who threw the gun outside the truck; there was no denying that. They asked me to get up, slowly, telling me if I moved fast, they would shoot low.

Terrified as heck, I could not believe that following the wrong crowd had actually gotten me into this situation. There was no turning back. Crying or pleading would not help the situation. We wanted to be the big dogs and that was the ticket we cashed.

Everyone else was asked to get up and sit back in the truck. I was the only one still lying flat. I asked the officer if I could get up. He looked at me and asked, "Sir, are you serious? You just had a gun and threw it out of a moving vehicle. You are being taken in."

It all hit me at once: what is my aunt going think? It felt like a bad dream that I couldn't wake up from. My heart was racing as fast as my mind, I felt sick, and I was having trouble breathing. It felt like an anxiety attack. I begin to panic; I could not believe I was on my way to juvenile detention.

As I sat in the patrol car, watching the police write citations and take reports, my homeboys just sat in the truck. I knew they were going to let me go without explaining or taking some responsibility. I sat in that car for about thirty minutes. I cried buckets of tears and was so nervous I urinated.

After we finally left the scene, things did not get better. We hadn't even gotten to detention and I asked the officers what must have been over 100 questions. They lost patience and finally told me to be quiet. Their response was: "Everything will be explained once you get to detention." I sat at the patrol station for almost 4 hours, and all I remembered was all the talks my brothers had with me about slowing down and putting the gang stuff to the side, my aunt fussing at me about getting my act together, being a good student, and to stop running with the wrong crowd. This was a reality hit.

After hours of sitting, I was formally charged with a Class A Misdemeanor for a Minor in Possession of a Firearm. It was close to midnight when I was checked into Juvenile Detention. As

I entered the cold cell, no bigger than my home bathroom, I was amazed that it had gone this far. All the games were over.

I hadn't spoken with anybody, but I thought about everyone. I thought about my dad a lot while I was in juvenile. I cried, prayed, and began to wonder if this was the end of everything. I wondered if bad decisions at seventeen would ever allow me to be productive again. I was placed on 48-hour lockdown since I was new to the unit. I got no sleep the first night; I felt claustrophobic and closed in, with no roommate, just one small window that gave me a view of the county jail and some traffic that passed down the busy street.

At six a.m. it was time for Roll and Breakfast Call. The unit was woken up and people were let out, one-by-one, to take medicine or receive their tray. The orange jumpsuits still felt like a dream. The guard on duty that morning was cool; he answered a lot of my questions, and even gave me some positive vibes about my charge and how things would be for the remainder of my stay. Saturday evening came and I was pissed that I was stuck in this small cell. The 48-hour lockdown was serious, and they could care less if you did not like it. All they cared about was compliance. I didn't want to test them; honestly,

I wasn't even that bad of a guy. I just wanted to be home.

I remember talking to the other juveniles, across the hall, under the doors, and through the walls; everyone had something to say to the new guy. The youth in there had major charges, more serious issues then mines. Everybody had a different opinion: "You got to do six months here, or 90 days. You may go to DYS, if you get one of the cool judges, she will let you go home on probation." All of these guesses began to bother me, I had messed up and felt that I was not going make it in there.

Visitation time came and my aunt was there. I remember being shackled and walked down the long hallway, nervous as heck, imagining what her remarks would be. I walked in the room and she walked up to hug me, tears in her eyes, and simply said, "I knew this was going happen, son. You don't listen."

My heart dropped and I began to cry. In that very sad moment, all of her guidance and speeches surfaced in my mind. We had a rough relationship through my early teens; I didn't want to listen. I was stubborn and determined to do what I wanted. We sat down as she dried her tears. She started to speak to me about the phone call, and her being worried sick after the police contacted her. When they arrest a juvenile, they have to contact your parent or guardian.

She asked me to explain, so I did. She began to fuss, but nothing said was short of the truth "I told you to stop following those crowds, and getting involved with that street mess." So much that took place at that event: a bullet grazed someone, guns were found in traffic stops, and someone had been run over. She said the story was put in the newspaper and was on the news the night prior.

I could hardly believe it. I had wanted the media attention that my brother, T. Lee had, but I never imagined it would happen like this.

Court was set for Monday morning at nine. My aunt began to pray while visitation was coming to a close and spoke encouragement to me about the upcoming court date. Walking away from visitation, and not being able to go home with her was the hardest thing yet. That Sunday was a better than the past couple days, but still hard. And now, I was even more anxious as Monday came closer. I was still thinking about the possibility of not going home.

All I could think about was worst case scenarios. At that time, crime had increased in the city and there were deaths daily. I figured because of that

I'd have to stay longer. One month away from my eighteenth birthday, and I faced the possibility of being in juvenile longer, being charged as an adult, and possibly losing the next few months to a year behind bars. This changed my entire perception and outlook on life. I began to tell myself, if I could only escape this issue, I would never turn back.

Seven on Monday morning came and I was more nervous and anxious than I had been in my entire life. I was told the judge could run behind because Mondays were always busy. Lock-ups from Wednesday of the week before had to be seen that next Monday morning. Court was pushed back.

I remember getting my name called to take that long walk to the courtroom, we sat on the opposite side of the building and had to be shackled and placed in a specific area prior to entering the courtroom. The guard that morning encouraged and motivated me, honestly God knew to put that brother in place over the weekend I was in.

The bailiff standing by the door called me in to the courtroom. "Lorenzo P. Lewis. Please enter the court room." All while being walked in by the guard, I saw my aunt and uncle sitting behind the prosecuting attorney and public defender; I had been told all weekend it would be beneficial to get this judge. She might show some mercy. Her reputation was a sincerity for wanting to help youth.

They went on with the proceedings and the story, it sounded horrible on paper; they read all my demographics and background information. It was still like a dream, I continued to ask myself, "Is this really happening?"

They decided to let me go home because my aunt agreed to have a steady watch on my whereabouts. I promised to be back in court in the next few months, and have check-ins every week with a probation officer. I could not leave the house unless I was with a parent. The restrictions were hard, but I was going home! I was so relieved.

I was ready to get back to the streets, to hear what was being said, and was wondering who had called and checked on me. I was told to have no contact with the guys I had got in trouble with, one of the few things that lingered my mind is that none of them came with me. This changed my perspective: the story can alter when it comes to systematic measures. I stated I was the one who was passed the gun after it was pulled on that young lady, but since I was the one to have possession, I was the only one to go to detention. I was put in a space of distrust, betrayal, and reality. I became a different young man in seventy-two hours.

That experience changed my life forever. I was spared, blessed, and given another chance. God saw different in this situation.

Cool Down

Life will spare you sometimes, won't it? We have all have gotten in some weird situations where we didn't think that things would really go left. And then they did go left. We have to sit back and gauge who we are becoming and ask ourselves is this the lifestyle I really want? I can tell you one thing, while being in that gang I knew that crap wasn't right, and more times than not it seemed useless and a huge waste of time. That gut instinct allows us to know what is right and wrong. We just have to move along with doing the right thing and forgiving ourselves for what we can't change.

I was battling with identity and wanting to be accepted. Just like most young African American males at age seventeen are truly battling find their mojo and exploring who they ultimately will become. This also goes to show you that having a support system and/or mentors are powerful. So, you have to be willing to forgive the process and path you are traveling.

Forgiveness: Forgiving ourselves for who we use to be is by far one of the most difficult processes. You may have been this person, or experienced some crazy stuff in one part of your life, but also may have rehabilitated or worked to become someone different. It's okay. Forgive yourself and tell yourself that you are still worth it, regardless of who you may have become in that process. When I got incarcerated, all I could think of was those brothers that I was running with could care less if I went down or not; they were glad they didn't and moved on with their life and own set of experiences. I knew I needed to get out the gang before it was too late, and when we know that it's time for us to change gears—no excuses—we should absolutely do it.

Do I wish to change my circumstances of being a juvenile delinquent and entering the same place that I was once born in? No. Being a part of the juvenile justice system right before graduating high school helped shape me to become the man I needed to become. I wouldn't have appreciated my life, would have taken school for granted, and wouldn't value having clean water at home, food in the cabinets, and clothes on my back. We tend to get acclimated to what we take for granted. So, making a decision to combat the luxury of your daily life puts you in a position to truly learn from it and get better from the process. Forgive yourself first and keep pushing.

Go Fast. But Not Too Fast: Sometimes in life we are so busy trying to keep up with the crowd and we lose ourselves while trying to navigate the crowd. Take a minute to slow down and really gauge the process by asking yourself these questions when making a decision to do something different or unusual from your routine:

Is the event or situation something that makes me feel good at the moment or the long term?
Will this situation or life circumstance not be cool to me once I get older or as I get older will this be funny to me?

Would the people around me, that love me, still be happy for me If I made this decision?

By asking yourself these few questions, you probably got your thumb twiddling and thoughts really flowing. By just slowing down and asking yourself these powerful questions you can really decide if that action is the right thing for you. You have to be real with yourself and be careful about everything you engage in. Life will shake you up sometimes, and although you are human, and yes you will overcome, some mistakes we make will mess up our lives up completely. we should never knowingly put ourselves in that type of situation.

Accept the Challenge; And Change:

After being released from juvenile, I went back to school to see my peers and everyone that had heard about the trouble I got into, I felt ashamed and guilty. I was more scared of what the people I knew since childhood and my extended family would think of me. I had all these thoughts in my head, and I can't say my fears weren't justified. Despite all that, I can tell you, the challenge you will go through won't be the easiest at first, but the change that comes along with that challenge will help you to become the best version of yourself. We already have the change inside of us, and sometimes going through tough situations will give us the push to change us completely.

Don't shy away from the challenge, you are going through your issues for a reason; the change is near. Catch it. Hold It. Embrace It!

Chapter 4
Drum Roll

I despised probation. The calling to check in regularly, the court assessed monthly fee, curfew orders, and the potential for a house monitor. But, thank God, they changed their mind. This lesson showed me how alone I was. My overwhelming feelings were bigger than a misdemeanor gun charge. The consequences of that charge had now had become a burden and a strain on my life. This made me realize, again, the change I had to make for my life; I had a decision period to see if this was the way I wanted to live. I had to make an abrupt decision between street life or making something out of myself.

This was a period in my life where I became closer to God and family, I saw the value in what I had, and how bad things could have been. I prayed that my heart would develop love and prosperity. The reality of having come close to killing someone scared me. I was moments from throwing my life away, summer was almost over, and reaching my eighteenth birthday on criminal charges was a heck of a milestone to remember. I challenged myself to think and engage better, to want better out of life, and to love and cherish the people around me better.

At eighteen years old I realized how short life really was. A lot of the homies and friends I ran with the year before were getting locked up, some were a part of more violence. The rest were dying. I figured out there was light on the other side of the tunnel. Senior year was here, and I was eighteen going on forty. My beard was growing; I had bass in the voice, and began to build a nice size to my frame after a summer of hitting the weights with the football pre-camp.

My style was become similar to my father. I wore loud colored shirts and had to have the nicest shoes and jewelry. I was drawn to fashion and the current trends. Every dollar I touched that summer got spent on clothes for school, definitely young man syndrome. I had to be seen and had to have attention. I was embarrassed to be approaching my last year of high school going on nineteen years old. It was as embarrassing as that seventh-grade moment.

I also remembered how blessed I was to be entering school that year. I was grateful to not be in juvenile or being held on charges. I had made it to my last year of school; I was gaining some traction, but had much work to do. A call to the school counselor's office was normal by this point; they were trying to figure out the status of my probation period, the issue from the year before, and switching me to another class. I ran with the Bloods in school and since I was not allowed any contact with them, I needed to be in class with different students. There was always some kind of issue when it came to gang stuff.

We definitely put ourselves out there as targets, and the more I think on it, I'm glad to realize there was no lasting significance in those street gangs and private cliques.

The recommendation was made that I finish my senior year out at an accelerated learning center due to my lacking academic performance. Switching schools and poor performance was going to put me back by another year. That would have me finishing high school at twenty. I wasn't having it. But I followed the recommendations of my counselor and made the switch. I was losing my senior experience, as well as the possibility of attending prom and being able to play football my last year of school.

This had to be a decision made on the spot. I knew that doing another year of school was not an option as a twenty-year-old black male. After my weekend of being in juvenile, I knew I wanted better and was serious about pursing my dreams of going to college. I began an accelerated school to finish closer to on-time. The new schedule required me to be at school a minimum of four hours per day and I could work if necessary. The model of the institution was to help those who were behind or for early parents, basically people in extreme situations.

Most of the population of this school was older and had begun living adult life while at this institution. This gave me motivation to grow up. I was able to work part of the day and attend school without receiving a bad report. I was driving myself to school by this point. I had begun to pay some of my own bills, and my uncle saw the transition and the way that I was able to adapt. I was off to being a man before my own eyes.

My work ethic grew tremendously at that point. More responsibilities meant more financial gain, so I picked up a second job to help support my habit of shopping. Working these two jobs this molded me in such way as to always have a hard-working spirit. I loved a paycheck and I saw the real value in working for your own money. The street life made no sense to me at this point, I figured I could work hard and get the same value. It took longer, but I could harvest the same fruit as others.

The year was winding down and I was at a steady pace. I had begun dating really heavily at this point. I felt as if I was so much older because of my lifestyle of work and school. I liked mature women, and I valued women who appeared to have real worth. Career, occupation, and a car were a plus in dating. I felt that I could not relate with girls of my own caliber, I even took a sophomore in college to prom with me. I felt that the bar had been raised and keeping up was a part of the regimen. I was able to participate in senior activities, but it felt odd, I felt older and more advanced. I worked as hard as my other classmates, went and came when I wanted, I dated older women, and I was beginning to sneak in the nightclubs.

Weeks out from graduation, I was on my last two courses, and I had to be down to one course to walk with my class. All the courses were synchronized through electronic applications, so I mostly sat in front of a computer with a facilitator in the class. I had gotten down to the last course, which was Algebra. I hated math. Having this as my last class was a nightmare and I was nervous as graduation came closer. This was an adventure because my aunt and uncle were still in doubt. They were still having issues adjusting to the current situation, feeling as if I regressed or went back to my old lifestyle.

Convincing them I was done was still an uphill battle, which was not made easier by my tendency to date older women and sneak into clubs. I had to show results; their biggest fear was me not finishing high school, getting lost to the streets, and becoming a part of the urban destruction.

Aunt Daisy was always reminding me, "I told your daddy on his death bed, 'I'm a get him out of school if I have to fight for him.'" She had done just that. All the way back to the third grade, going through issues of retention in middle school, and my lack of focus in high school, she never gave up, she was my biggest fan. I had big shoes to fill; they always said you are our last investment. All of their kids had gone through their process, and I believe they felt with me they could do things differently and see me actually complete school and achieve success.

With four days left, I had the hardest time passing the quizzes and test required. I felt stuck, I got frustrated, I felt that I would not get past this module and be done. I could still walk, but would have to return the next year to finish the last class. I gave this course all I had, and I continued to fail. I would not give up. I kept going and pushing through the failures. I did not let this module hold me up from my parents being proud of me. The next few days, I was the first student in the lab and the last to leave. I was determined to be finished before graduation.

We graduated on a Thursday evening. I will never forget the time: it was 4:45pm CDT. My heart began to race, my was sweat beaming and my palms were sweaty. Graduation was at seven that evening. I was on my last test, and I failed it several times. I remember taking a walk outside, praying and pacing, asking God to come through, I was so close to the finish line. I wanted to receive my diploma like all my fellow classmates.

I had a cousin who was very close that graduated in the same class as me. She was graduating with honors and I didn't want to be the one who didn't make it out. All the odds were stacked against me after the past few years. I knew that change was in place and I had to push through to see the fruit that was in my path.

At 5:35 p.m. I submitted my last answer to the quiz. I passed right at 72 percent! I was so excited I had finished all of my coursework as a high school senior. This moment showed me much about consistency and perseverance, not to ever give up, so you can stay on course with your dreams. This was milestone for sure. Being nineteen years old and walking the stage with my diploma in a few hours was a feeling that I could not describe. I fought hard; I went through a lot in the years before. I went home and burst into tears on my Aunt Daisy, hugging her neck as tightly as possible, crying real tears of joy and happiness. We met the goal.

That morning before I left home, I remember getting my clothes prepared for graduation. I was determined to finish; God had walked me through the trials, and at seven, on the evening of June 6, 2007, I was a graduating senior with a high school diploma. I survived the streets, the doubts of not making it, the learning disadvantages they say I had, my mother and father not being present, and being away from my siblings. Juvenile delinquency did not hold me back. All of this was done with the support of my aunt and uncle and with much eagerness to see the results of achievement. This was, and would continue to be, my testimony.

Cool Down

When will the drums stop beating? I'm sweating bullets just thinking about making it to the finish line. Will I ever make it? How long will the race continue? These are the thoughts running through my head as I prepare to move past the drum roll. The results on the other side of the beat always leave me in a doomed state of mind. One thing is for sure: we've got to either progress or move backwards. And, anything but going backwards is always my personal motto.

When I think of pushing forward, I'm reminded of this early 2000s rap single, "No Rearview" by Memphis Rapper StarLito ft Don Trip. That hit they dropped was real medicine during my time of overcoming. For those of us who are always facing some type of adversity or issues, we all are experiencing an urge to focus on what we can't change: the past. To keep us in the present, remember there is a period to every sentence and an ending to every storm. Your life has probably brought major difficulties, and at times you didn't know if you would get through the last drumroll—but you did!

Take a Deep Breath.

No matter how you may think you are going through your day-to-day, life will always throw you some mess that you may or may not be prepared for. We must remember to take a moment and take a deep breath. During my time of needing to finish my test hours to get the green light to graduate, I took some time to breathe, relax, and take a moment. I checked in with God and asked him for the support that I knew I needed; we can't fight our battles alone.

Your higher source and support around you will be the reason you make it. We just weren't built to take on everything alone. We need the support, so always tap into your source to get replenished. More energy will increase your results. Deep breathing techniques really helped me out during that moment before graduating. Breath work didn't stop the time or the finish line requirement, but by taking a moment to breath and re-group I was able to find the balance and energy needed to keep going. I learned that by getting in your quiet place, closing your eyes, and using soft music or complete silence to relax is a gamechanger!

Believe and Be Aware...

I know there are things I am simply not the best at doing or completing. I struggle with math, sentence structure, and keeping my cool. Because I realize my weakness, I am that much better. Becoming self-aware and understanding your highs and lows makes a difference. Let's be frank, there are some things you have simply failed at and have run away from making right all together. So, make a plan to map out how to tackle that fear and making things right. You can do anything imaginable; you are worthy; don't ever forget that!

You Haven't Arrived, but you did Make It…

Choose to be upbeat about the process of life; we all need to have goals and ideals aspire for or want to achieve. And when working so hard towards finishing something almost takes the life out of us, we cry a river once we get there. Yes, you have made it, but there is much more to do! One thing that came to me after getting through high school was realizing there was much more I wanted to accomplish.

I could have stopped dreaming or chose not to want much more than to just go to college. Most of us will limit our beliefs and goal system once we hit that big mark, use that same energy and focus, and maximize your goals! As I stated before, realize there are some things that you are absolutely not good at—that's okay. One thing about being a first-generation college graduate was it was easy for me to become settled and relieved. We were all put here on earth to be great and create some of the world's greatest inventions and ideas. Keep your goals high, and don't let up from achieving them—not even if you fail while trying to do them!

Chapter 5
The Blocks

Leaving high school was a pleasure because I had overcome the hurt of circumstances and begun to walk in my true destiny. I realized without finishing high school my life would be literally in shambles.

At age of eighteen I had already finished more formal education than my natural parents. All the trials of my youth had become a testimony. I was applying for colleges and glad to be the man that I knew that I could be. I still had a chip on my shoulder, still unsatisfied at some of the boomerangs that life had thrown at me.

The bible states in Philippians 4:13, "I can do all things through Christ which strengthens me." This was my real power in the day and night. So, as I prepared for to apply for schools, I was unsure of how I would be admitted with a thirteen on the ACT.

This is embarrassing, but quite frankly I didn't try very hard and didn't pay much attention. So, the score wasn't exactly a surprise. I re-took the ACT and made a 14, just one-point difference.

I had my made my mind up about going to college and leaving Little Rock. I applied to all the local colleges: Grambling State and Southern University. I applied at a majority of the popular Historically Black College and Universities (HBCUs) like Morehouse and Clark Atlanta. DENIED was the reality; none of these institutions were taking a chance on me. My feelings were hurt and I had few resources to turn to. I didn't care to read very much and tutoring wasn't affordable. I was tired of scraping by on my minimum wage salary to pay for the ACT again.

I kept hearing, "Apply to University of Arkansas at Pine Bluff (UAPB); you can make it on the YARD!" I kept applying to all the predominantly white institutions (PWIs) and the popular HBCUs not thinking about the work that my peers put in to get into these schools.

I finally applied to UAPB after more than ten rejection letters. I remember it clear as day, getting that letter in the mail. Moms had called me to say I had some mail waiting on the kitchen table, and I swiftly made it home. The return address said UAPB Office of Admissions, my sweat was beaming, I knew this could be it before I had to go to the local community college. I opened it and read the letter: I declare you to be admitted on conditional admission.

My heart paused. This language was quite different, so it took a minute to take it all in. I was excited, but wanted to understand what they meant, so I called the number listed. My question was, "Have I been admitted? Can you explain this language of 'conditional?'" The representative in the admissions office told me I had been admitted, but I would be on academic watch for the first year. I was going to college.

All I could imagine was being away from home and being able to say that I'm a student at an HBCU, this was the epitome of DOPE. It could not get any better; I had made it to the pinnacle. I think I told everybody during the next month. The thoughts of dorm life, late night parties, traveling, and being able to pledge a fraternity ran through my mind. This was all becoming a reality. The only thing I wasn't taking in context was actually doing the work of being a working college student. That was the challenge that I was up against.

Freshman move-in was near, and I remember working so hard at Wendy's to have enough income to be dressed every day that semester. Those were the good holidays; I linked up with a few buddies from high school that were attending as well. We still had that high school mindset, thinking about whom could stand out or getting the best-looking woman on campus.

These are the days now we laugh about. We talked about becoming "The Chic Magnet," a term that was defined by the Houston sensation, rapper Paul Wall. His chic magnet was an eye catcher to every woman and a real womanizer. I was all in. This chic magnet movement was something serious. Going into college was a new environment, and while I knew there would be different adventures, my woman crazy self was focused on being able to meet women from coast to coast. I thought of it like the ball was in my court. Imagine this one chubby guy, who dressed really nice, with expensive sneakers, and $30 haircuts. This was the recipe for being the chic magnet. My focus on women instead of school caused me to fail classes and miss a bunch of school.

I'll never forget my first girlfriend on the yard. She was a southern woman from Memphis. What started as a mind-blowing experience quickly turned into the worst. I learned I could not maintain a girlfriend and go to school. My lack of experience in high school was obvious. I always say that college made me into a MAN. I was able to come and go as I pleased, meet and greet others, build culture and network with those likeminded, provide financially for myself, and not be monitored by my parents. The experience was deeper though; I was gaining friends and allies for a lifetime.

Despite my growth, I didn't know how to treat a woman; I was never taught how to be good to someone that liked you. Be mindful my aunt was the epitome of a great woman, but growing up with many brothers and male figures around, I was never actually shown how to treat and be with a woman. As young men we have to be around those who model good relationships. Without these figures there can be many issues and obstacles in the girlfriend and boyfriend business. We broke up after a month.

By the next month I was with someone else, and that only lasted for two weeks. I dated like that for a while. I felt like I had to make up for what was lost when I was just twenty years old. This finally took a toll on my social interactions with women. I began to disrespect and mistreat women.

My aunt and uncle had a stable relationship, but did not expose us to how they built and maintained it. Not exposing your youth to those conversations can be very detrimental. I grew up having to learn the hard way in relationships, and eventually through a mentor. Having mentors and those around you who care is abundance! I was blessed to have some close friends I classified as brothers around me. These friends were the definition of committed and always stood in the gap when needed. My undergraduate career was an altering experience; it was where I developed the masculine traits that I demonstrate today.

I define manliness as a set of attributes, behaviors, and roles generally associated with boys and men, mostly defined as socially and biologically created. I had become socially dominant within my peer group. I was viewed as the brother with the outspoken voice and as a leader. I had no idea the torch would soon be passed. The lord had ordained this way before my realization and the real work was ready to be done My father also possessed such dominance in character, integrity in soul, and hardworking ethic, whether his life was ideal or not. One missing component of my maturity was my faith.

During the dormitory years I was blessed to have a childhood friend there, a good brother who was focused on giving his life to the lord and living out his late old man's dreams of being a vessel of salvation and change, and preaching the gospel.

The conversations with us started to shift, "Hey Zoe? You believe in God? What's your stance with getting saved? Have you given your life to Christ yet?" I didn't have answers for him. These were serious questions coming from a close friend as I sat on my small twin bed in Johnson Hall of the Harold J. Complex at The University of Arkansas at Pine Bluff. I began to lie, and then my mouth became glued shut. The spirit of God wasn't going allow me to make up this lie.

A long pause was next. I began to utter, "Well, brother I think I have." The room was silent as my good friend and I locked eyes for thirty seconds or more. I began to state that I would like to know more, but would like to have the conversation another time, my cricket cellular device showed it was roughly fifteen minutes to six and the café was closing soon.

I said, "Hey brother, let's go eat. Pocket's low and we spent a good grip of petty cash that week on the 99 cents menu at McDonald's." So, we went to fill our wide bellies and look at the pretty girls prance through the cafeteria on campus. I felt convicted by our last prior conversation and stated to my good brother, "Man, I need to be saved. Bro, I hate to leave this world tonight and not know where I need to go."

His face turned red, his cheekbones said it all as he smiled from ear to ear. "My friend Zoe, I got you and I'm glad to know that you want to turn your life over to the lord."

I was excited and nervous all at the same time. The spirit had convicted me, and for a young brother as myself, growing up with a praying auntie and strong Baptist background, I felt as the roots of my beginning could now spark. I realized that the power of the Holy Spirit and the way I wanted to live my life righteously was coming together.

Tears began to roll down my cheeks as I sat there with all the other students eating dinner that day in the café; I turned my back towards the crowd and thanked the Lord. My heart was filled with joy, anxiety, and excitement. I knew no one forced this decision, but I made it by myself to give my life over to Christ. I began reading the bible and praying more, my good brother introduced me to a great pastor back home, who led a powerful church and spoke a good work about the gospel.

As normal, we came home to Little Rock on a Friday evening to see our natural circle and friends after a long week- of studying and skipping classes when we had to.

My good brother said "How about we meet with this pastor of mines who changed my life this evening at 6:00pm Chili's restaurant for some appetizers?"

I was hesitant, as I knew that there could be a major shift in conversation due to my recent decision of seeking salvation. I agreed to meet up at six to meet and share good conversation.

When the waiter asked where we preferred to sit, I blurted out first, "Is there any seating towards the back of the place?"

The pastor gave me a grin-look and laughed while stating, "You must get a lot to talk about young man."

We all chuckled, but with the seriousness of conversation that would take place I needed a safe and comfortable place. We laughed, and talked as we ate salty chips and red salsa. We talked about how college life was treating us.

The pastor asked, "So I hear that there is something you want to talk to me about?" He said, "I want you to be completely comfortable and honest about what it is, that I'm a man and every man is equal under the level of God."

I paused because his approach was so warming and not aggressive. I shared with him about me wanting to get saved. He said that you have made the first step by speaking this into fruition and followed by mentioning this scripture: Ephesians 4:15 "but speaking the truth in love, we are to grow up in all aspects into Him who is the head, even Christ."

My heart was beating out of my chest, but I felt the same emotion that I experienced in the cafeteria that day. My spirit allowed me to know that God was present and to move onward and forward in his kingdom.

The pastor asked me when I was ready to be saved and I asked him when the best time was. He said, "Time waits for no one. We only experience short notice in this earthly form."

We continued eating our appetizers. As we left the restaurant there were good vibes, healthy conversation, and the spirit of the Holy Ghost present in all two hours. It began to rain; it had been very cloudy and fog was forming in the atmosphere.

Upon leaving, the pastor shook my hand and said, "Young man, I can't leave this restaurant without knowing your heart is in the place of Jesus." He stated that he could do it right then and there, in that parking lot, and the baptism would take place shortly after. I had attended his church a few times in the past and he had remembered me. He wanted to make sure that this process could be sacred for all of us.

So, on a cold day in December 2009, in the Chili's parking lot, I committed myself to Christ. I had begun to run my race with Christ, knowing that the finish line could seem far away or that there may be plenty of hurdles or faster runners besides me. My life could be a real race of happiness, triumph, and even pitfalls. Once committed to working for Jesus Christ, all wouldn't be so cheesy and blooming. The real test was near and God was continuing to prepare me.

Being a twenty-year-old black man attending a HBCU college, with many barriers in my lane, it was only a matter of time before my real faith would be tested. I was ready to go forward and ecstatic at the thought of what possibly could be near. I was prepared to run my RACE.

Cool Down

Getting on the right track is never easy…

Sometimes making the decision to do the right thing will be harder than what you can imagine. I thought making the right decisions was simple? Actually, making the steps in the right direction can even be difficult. I was beginning to think that in my 20s that I would be unable to make these smart and critical decisions. Your life circumstances will test you, and yes, I was tested time and time again.

We all are tested, but how we move forward and press through the mark, the race of life, so we can be emotionally free. The transition to college, being woman crazy, and giving my life to Christ was simply not an easy thing to digest. But that's life for you—a rollercoaster. I am sure, that even when our heart and desire is on the right thing, outside forces—whether negative or positive—will persist and pour their way into our space. We have to choose optimism and never give up on our process. Appreciate the things that life is throwing at us as we strengthen that emotional muscle.

Build Your Emotional Muscle…

I wanted the best out of life, and I realized that after taking the ACT over and over again, low score after low score, denials after denials. I was tired of this, but there was something that would not let me give up. Emotional Muscle, the force that lies inside of us all, gets tested over and over again, will throw us for a loop. We still can't give up. When we are rejected and looking for a certain response to make us happy or help us to reach our mark, and continue to be told no, our emotions and head is all messed up.

It's hard to keep pressing through. When we start to build this muscle, our heart become less weary and we begin to build a tolerance for rejection. Even then, I realized that with a low score on my ACT, barely a 1.9 GPA, and being a juvenile offender even some of the Historically Black College and Universities (HBCUs) wouldn't take a chance on me.

Each time I received a letter of rejection I would get in my quiet place for a few moments, recite to myself the "These Days Shall Pass" talk about how it would get better, and go after it again. All this to say I was building my emotional muscle. Once we get in our quiet place, and think over the rejection or circumstance while visualizing and embracing that things would get better, it will get better.

Next time, you are thrown off and rejected just remember your emotional muscles are getting stronger and eventually you will find your success.

Glad I Made It Right and You Can Too…

I couldn't believe that I would ever revisit the thought of believing in GOD. Seriously, I grew up with a bunch of believers and family that talked about the Church, and Jesus, and didn't stick with me when I needed them the most.

It's a similar story to many young brothers and sisters out there. We may have grown up with a pretty strict spiritual background, (ex: praying grandmother, uncle served on the deacon board, etc.) But there may have been a re-direction as life kept pressing forward or maybe faith became not so important due to all the other life things that start to pop-up (figuring out personal identity, social media, etc.). However, once our paths become so departed from the right source, and that's GOD/Higher Power, we can feel the resistance. I knew to pray, and be involved in the word, but I just went my own direction. Honestly, after my family stopped attending church as much in my late-teens I think everybody in my circle just went their own direction.

To this day, I am so thankful for my great friend and brother Earl for not giving up on me and pointing me in the right direction. How do we realign ourselves to get reconnected with our higher source? This process may be different for everybody, but in all ways we all have to believe that nothing in this world, our passion or greatest fears can be conquered alone. You just can't put any high priority on any body or object. It's a matter of repositioning and getting back to where you can be centered on all things that will make you balanced in your physical, emotional, and spiritual being.

There may be some adjustments that need to be made in your circle. Consider using powerful breathing techniques or cycles of meditation with soft music or quietness to let your thoughts settle. There is power in just being alone and getting centered emotionally.

When I started to read the Bible when I felt scared and nervous about being saved, I realized that the fear was coming from a place of inconsistency. The fact that I stopped attending church with family as much and no one ever clearly stated why, always made me think that it was okay to stop believing in GOD and stop attending a worship center, which clearly was not true. We are rooted in habit and belief, first and foremost. How we feel and believe about something determines our results.

It's important that we get in our quiet place and think and search for that feeling of discouragement that you may be feeling. Once you are able to obtain that feeling, start to process it by asking yourself why you feel like this? Can it be changed? Does it involve me talking with someone from my past to help overcome this feeling? Start to take some of these steps and process. Once you're spiritually aligned, your life will begin to prosper. Mines did and yours will too. You are going HIGHER!

Chapter 6
"The Hard Shift"

After experiencing college for a while, life seemed to have come to fruition. I was finally able to learn the groove of campus, professors, and the food wasn't so bad for an overpriced meal plan without the dormitory stay. I had gotten to mid-point of college, I was still breathing, no wounds, and STDs hadn't caught up with me yet, so I was doing just fine.

Being a tender boy from Little Rock, with high ambition, but no means of direction, I was happy to be just living. I was overworked for sure; I worked heavy hours at Popeye's Chicken, and from time to time I would go back to Little Rock to wait tables at a local café hosted in a senior's facility. That was the real bread and butter: the loving and sweet elders would hook my pockets up and give me dope inspiration for going back to school after work in the senior's cafeteria.

I remember this sweet, elderly white lady by the named of Jo. She was like the grandmother I never had. She would fuss at me for being the best me, give me a little gas money, and even would invite me over to her place to tell me long stories of her late husband who served in the Vietnam War. According to Jo, being widowed was the life to be living. Often times, she would tell me to always be the best version of me, and that I would someday climb the corporate ladder of success. She was roughly 6', with a limp in her walk, and medium white gray hair. She always smelled as good as a dozen roses. She gave me twenty-one-year-old me the love and sincerity that my actual grandmother wasn't able to give to me, I always adored her for the affection she displayed. It was during this time that I moved out of the dorms.

Sharing an apartment with a close friend from home was a bomb idea. We had two bedrooms, a nice dining area, and the bills were super reasonable for two young brothers who barely made $10.00 an hour. I can remember being on public assistance for our utilities, even with two jobs. The food stamps were cool too. We couldn't wait till the fifth of the month to fill the cabinets up. Those were the good days; we struggled, but learned the value of really working to have something. I must say that I'm a product of public assistance and the humility I gained is irreplaceable.

Growing up without my biological mother was confusing sometimes, and was even more so as I suppressed the emotions that I should have been experiencing. I always mentioned that I had a mother and father figure, but not my actual mother and father. This distinction helped me put off the reality. The reality was I really wanted that relationship, and I had a bunch of questions and thoughts that should have been answered. I remember Christmases and birthdays when she didn't even call. I wouldn't say she didn't care.

As I got older, I realized she must have hated to not raise me. Randomly I would get calls from her to check in; the conversations would always end in emotion and crying on the other end of the telephone. I never questioned why she couldn't be around, partly because my Aunt Daisy was honest about what was happening in my biological mother's life. I hardly ever held much anger towards her. If anything, I was apathetic when we talked. I was thankful because she gave me human life, and when we did talk it was always love, for sure. I even visited her and the Lewis family in Mobile, Alabama a few times as a youngster. The last good conversation I had with my mother she spoke of how she wanted to see me succeed.

She visited me in Arkansas when I was about fifteen; she stayed about a week. We had a good time. We shared priceless conversation and went through some emotions of how life could have been different for the both of us. She told me something very sacred, and I will never forget that moment. It was about two in the morning, and the house was quiet as a mouse. I heard this hysterical scream and chanting in the next room.

I woke up quickly, and my heart felt as it had fallen through my stomach, as I threw the sheets from off the bed to run in the next room. My mother was up praying and speaking in tongues, thanking the good Lord above. I was really confused and didn't understand what was taking place. I didn't know if this was a joke or maybe actions from being on some kind of substance.

I listened as she yelled to the top of her lungs, talking to our maker about the vision that she saw, and how she was sorry for her life going the way it did. In all my years of living I had never seen something so vivid and raw besides seeing someone in the Baptist Church catch the Holy Spirit during praise and worship. She stated that her vision was to see me excel and that I would be something really important.

Tears began to flow from my face, and she beat her hands on the ground, and yelled "Jesus, comes do your will." My palms were sweating and my heart was thundering. I was stunned at what was taking place. She stated that I was the special child out of all my other siblings. I think the world of all my siblings, so I don't really agree with this, but I always say she was having an out of body experience, and God was working with her to reveal some things. It was some years after that moment before I would hear from her again. Our relationship went back to what it was, and thoughts, perceptions and emotions were suppressed and forgotten.

I remember quitting my job at Popeye's Chicken and getting to work as a packing receiver for Tysons Chicken, it was almost double the pay. It had good benefits, but the 12-16-hour shift, every other day, was hard. There were long hours in the freezer, heavy loads of chicken, and short breaks to get back to the below freezing of being a work slave on the evening shift.

This was the new phase of being an adult; it was an advantage that before I left college, I knew the real essence of working hard and supporting my own household. My aunt and uncle were merely an hour away; I had my own vehicle and paid my own insurances and utilities. I was living the good, but realistic life. It was normal that we got off work at about two in the morning and went in the afternoon.

This particular night felt different, we actually got off a bit later, so it was closer to three. My white shirt was dirty and sweaty, and I had cottonmouth from being on the line. I was ready to pack it in for a good night's sleep.

Early in morning of August 2009 I received a phone call that would change my life. I remember the phone rang as loud as noon hour bell would in New York City. I jumped up from my bed, feet dangling from the side of the bed post, and slowly put the phone up to my warm ears and immediately heard a screeching scream yell into the telephone.

My heart dropped; my stomach felt as it was paper being twisted. The sweaty palms didn't make it a better. My sister yelled through the phone that at roughly eight that morning our mother passed. She had fallen sick months before and was in a nursing home rehabilitating from a light stroke.

My thoughts were racing and my body felt weak as I realized she had left this earthly life. To think that a twenty-one-year-old male wouldn't grow old knowing much about his natural parents was mind bothering. Time didn't have a place for us.

As I reflect over the moments of her leaving, what I could have done differently, or better, I am left wondering how could we been closer when she made a choice to not raise me. These are the things that made it rough and hard to accept over the next few weeks.

We made a long trip to Mobile, Alabama to memorialize my mother. This was one of the hardest times in my life, I was severely depressed and didn't know how to cope. I couldn't sleep well and had thoughts of wondering what if life just ended here.

I had one close friend that really stepped in to show support. She called and checked on me several times a day, talked to me before I went to sleep, and even came by to pick me up to just ride the city and talk things through. It was imperative to have the proper support group through the rough time of losing someone. At this time, I did not even think about therapy and how that could have made things better.

I wish I had because therapy was key in dealing with the loss of my father at eight-years-old. It truly helped me get through the battle of grief. The trip was filled with the memories I did have of my mother. My siblings weren't handling it well. Only three of us shared the same parents; my sister is a bit younger and my brother older than me. They took it really rough when we realized we were all that we had. We leaned on each other for guidance and support, but struggled because we all lived miles away from each other.

The day of the funeral was surrounded with grief and sorrow. I remember viewing my "old lady" and not bursting into tears; held up by my brother, I could feel the connection we shared from mother to son. Regardless of our separation, the connection was firm and spiritual.

Shortly afterwards, we gathered with family and spoke of all the good times, that was shared with my mother and others. She was known as a hustler and go-getter in the gritty streets of Mobile, Alabama. Between her and my pops they both had this hustler spirit about them. I see my drive and ambition as their legacy. During my tough time a few lines of Claudia Lee's poem, "Missing Mama" stayed on my heart and mind, "I awake each morning to start a new day but the pain of losing you never goes away. I go about the things I have to do and as the hours pass, I think again of you." It was a bit of peace in an emotional storm.

When I think about the death and the hardship I endured, I am reminded of an Olympic track race. I'm running a hard-felt race in life with many hurdles to success. Dealing with the loss of parents at such an early age gave me the inner strength needed to continue the race of life. I made a choice as a young man, with ambition and goals that I would get through this, that life doesn't end and the race doesn't stop here. If I run slow or am not in first place, it will not be a loss. I will stand. I will conquer. I will get over this hurdle of life. Momma I'm still missing you, but I will finish the race, I love you.

Your Son.

Cool Down

Losing any body close to you is rough. I can't fathom how to help others grieve. I wish it was simple as saying things will get better and it will. But, it doesn't.

Grief is a process. I can tell you, as a young black brother at the age of twenty-one, who had lost both parents, it was surreal. I wouldn't wish that on my worst enemy. But I'm also glad that I won't have to suffer that in my later life.

The truth behind this is we will bury our parents or loved ones, or they will be the ones putting us in the ground. The pain behind losing family is never easy. If I could have chosen to go before them, I would have chosen to go. Or, at least I would have preferred a deep sleep and not wake up till years later. Then the early emotion wouldn't have been so deep. But pain is a teacher, and I wouldn't be the man I am today without losing my mother.

A wise man always told me I am better because I did lose my mother. He stated that it's one less, painful experience to endure in life, because believe me we all will have to experience some painful stuff in life. I wish I could tell you we won't. You will make it though.

You Can't Be Prepared Enough…

People always ask me how to prepare for losing anyone close to you. I always tell them that grief is unexpected. I thought because I was not raised by mother it wouldn't have been that difficult. But it seemed more difficult because there are some missing parts to my life that I cannot address without her. I figured out the best way to find answers was to contact my family and siblings to better understand myself: past, present, and future. I found we had an unorthodox experience with our parents because they were incarcerated. But in any deceased or non-communicative relationship the best way is to forgive yourself first.

It's best to know that our experience, regardless of the severity, starts with forgiving self, and then forgiving them and the situation. I had every reason to be upset at my mother.) In each circumstance, I had to first forgive myself and then her. Although we are the author of our own story, sometimes we can't dictate or force time, especially when people leave us expected or unexpectedly shift. The way that you prepare for the small difficulties will be your extension towards the greater outcomes in the future.

Having Somebody Goes A Long Way…

There is power in numbers, as they say. The real power is just somebody who has your back; it doesn't have to be a whole crowd. I can remember that I was stressed to the max after losing my mother as a young brother with all of these questions and lack of relationship.

The strongest thing that I had was having someone in my corner, who could talk to me, believe in me, and push me. It was that one friend, Diana, that had my back and would stay on the phone with me all night because I was scared to go to sleep, because all I could do was dream of a funeral hearse and casket or the memories of my mother's hysterical outbreak at the house when she visited. Diana was so timely, and I am grateful that she had my back and best interest.

It is expected that when we lose somebody, or circumstances happen whether its separation or non-communicative experiences, we think that family is supposed to be and be the ones who stand in the gap. This is not always true.

I can recall there were many people around me when my mother passed, plenty of calls, house-visits, etc., but the attention and sincerity that I got from Diana was more than all of those one-off actions. She kept checking on me, asking the right questions, making sure that my energy was grand, and assuring to me that she had my back at all costs.

We all need somebody to help us during those rough experiences, but at the same time hold the righteous place of being loyal, committed, and sincere. Having the right support group will be magical in our place of darkness and overcoming pain.

Chapter 7
Fulfilling Purpose

That was a tough summer and the season of autumn was near. I kept pushing through the race even though sometimes I felt as if I was the only person that was walking through the storm of losing a parent. Despite those feelings, I knew in my head that I wasn't alone, but being a man with stoic character and image—5'8" and heavyset—brothers, I couldn't show any weakness nor cry.

I cultivated a sense of pride and dignity that summer. I became someone with an internal structure that could not be moved nor tampered with. I started to really invest in my inner-self and read more books then I had in my adolescence. I knew that by continuing to face tragedy with both parents gone, it was a matter of time before I became an author or someone that could give motivational speeches about "Being the Best You."

I saw this vision because of the mental toughness my story had developed in me. My story and my life were raw. The fact that I saw the potential did my heart good. I realized that regardless of the circumstance, with hard work and faith, I could still achieve my dreams. I conquered getting out of trouble as a juvenile and getting in to college. I knew even as a heavyset, young man from Arkansas, I could still be something, regardless of my story. I was motivated and I understood the meaning of perseverance. I had gotten enough teaching and life lessons to learn the value of perseverance.

I believe that many black men do not have enough mental and personal stamina to withstand the obstacles of life. There are many theoretical discussions and data that expose the struggle of our circumstances. The one thing that doesn't back that up is that we are some bad creatures that can stand the heat of a burning furnace. I tell you, if there is a will there is a way. I'll leave that with you because I believe it to be a true and divine statement. God makes a way, and with work, you can tap into power that lies in you.

It was time to register for college that semester. I had decided to move back to Little Rock, just 45 minutes away from where I attended school at the University of Arkansas at Pine Bluff. I needed a new beginning, my grades were less than stellar, and I was distracted due to all the social shifts that had taken place. Moving back to Little Rock made me feel revived and ready to make real effort this time around. I hadn't truly understood the value of education and didn't take it seriously. As I assessed my situation, I realized that all these student loans weren't going to disappear and I didn't have the financial means to pay out of pocket. I was borrowing money left and right just to get by in higher education. So, I took full advantage of the resources my school offered and attended a satellite location for UAPB. It was much smaller and there was not much eye candy floating around, but it worked.

As I looked for a better paying job, I remembered a friend I knew from the old neighborhood telling me about a juvenile detention center hiring. I was having flashbacks just thinking about it. I told myself there isn't no way in the hell, I'm going to go and work in some long and dark, bleach smelling hallway, with violent youth cursing and shaking the windows. I continued to fill out applications online to find a job, but there were no calls back.

As time went on, I was becoming impatient. "No one will hire my Black Ass," is what the little voice in my head was yelling. And I kept coming back to this job that paid $10.00 an hour. In 2009 that was some good money, really good money for someone who didn't even have his own place. I would be gaining financially, but I would have to face my past again. I would have to face the consequences and memories of a wild child who did not submit and follow instructions. I had the size and the swag to go along with this job. I was a former defensive lineman with a mouth full of gold. I took a chance and put in the application. I told myself, "They won't call back anyway. Right?"

Days passed by and I received an email from a weird email address: "Mr. Lewis, your application meets your requirements. We want to follow up with you. When is a good time to speak?"

My heart fell through my stomach. It was the Foot Locker gig I wanted! My mind was fixed on working in the mall, and I could cop the Jordan's that were dropping on the employee discount. But wait; there wasn't a Foot Locker logo on the email. But I needed a job, badly, because this low wage wasn't cutting it.

I wrote back and scheduled a phone call for the next evening. I knew it was time that I purchased my own vehicle and while school was going fair, the refund checks from financial aid weren't coming fast enough. I can remember watching that email list serve weekly to see if my name would show up for disbursement. They were the good ol' days, spending $2,000-3,000 on clothes, food, and trips to Memphis or Atlanta. My aunt always said, "Isn't nothing like a Negro with a check on a Friday night." And we were just that, young, in college, with more money than we could manage, and broke by the next Friday.

The time for the phone call was getting closer, and was all anticipation. "Hello," said the caller. "Mr. Lewis this is Mrs. Smith, Human Resource Director for Alexander Juvenile Detention in Saline County."

My heart beat even faster at this point; I scared the hell out of myself. They did actually call. We spoke about coming in for a face-to-face assessment and if I was interested in the position. I nervously agreed.

The weekend had passed, and it was time to go and speak to HR and the hiring team for the job at the juvenile detention facility. I built up courage to go, and besides, $10 an hour was hard to pass up.

I remember driving down a long, gravel road, lined with fields, as I drove up to the detention center. My leg was becoming stiff as I drove even further. You would have thought I was going to prom; I was so nervous.

Dark brick buildings and fenced bob wire were surrounded by acres of land. My Ford Ranger pulled up slowly to park; the brakes screeched and rocks were thrown as I put the pick-up in park, and my head sank in the pillow of the driver's headrest. I stepped out the vehicle, and took one deep breath as I began to walk up to the facility.

This detention center looked scarier than the one I was at. It was a much larger complex and there were guards all over, covering perimeters and gate points. I was asking myself if it was an adult jail. But no, it wasn't; it held some of the more serious juvenile offenders in the state for violent crimes. This was no longer just a job; this was a big deal.

As I sat in the lobby waiting for my name to be called, there were juveniles being walked in, some in shackles and some with officers walking behind them. It was much quieter than the juvenile I was in years before. The irony of all this was I was turning twenty-two in a few months, but I was just four years from being in the cage myself.

The assessment went well, and I was told that there would be a call if I was needed. Two days later, I was offered the job. My heart was full of excitement. God placed in me the desire to do work for his Kingdom. I would be in a place recently left, dealing with issues and conflict. I accepted the position to work at the detention center.

For the first time I had a pretty good job along with competitive benefits. This was a game changer! Despite my newfound commitment to school and faith and my new job, I couldn't shake the streets. I was back at home and knew the ins and outs of everything; I was beginning to figure out what everybody had been up to since high school was over. Some were off to college doing well; some were like me in school locally and just working a decent wage job. Others were dead or barely making it and life was beginning to get the best of them.

Real life had set in, and the fun, high school vibes were drifting away slowly. Little Rock has always been a bit of a college town, a place for out-of-towners to start a new path. Little Rock also had its share of street violence, gangs, and illicit activities. I found myself getting caught up in the havoc with old friends: Friday nights of clubbing, and local happy hours were working out pretty well for me. I was enjoying being legally able to go out in my city, and be out late with no repercussions.

A few semesters on the yard gave me some credibility with my aunt and uncle. I was able to buy my first 96' Chevy Caprice, or "Bubble Chevy" we call it. It had copper brown bucket seats with a quiet engine. I was able to give the Ford Ranger back to my uncle and drive my own vehicle.

I was a twenty-two-year-old with a factory, stock Chevy Caprice. As I drove the streets all eyes were on me, I got stopped left and right about selling it or answering questions about if the motor was pumped up. Police would follow me or pull me over because of the Chevy Caprice's reputation. I liked the positive and negative attention and couldn't get enough of it. I liked it so much my next move was to get the car re-painted and put some rims on it, so that it could stand out even more. Most of the Chevy's had their own identity and that how the drivers got a reputation. Fresh out the paint shop, it was a 24-karat gold paint job. The smell of fresh paint gave me the chills, and that beauty was all mine. Little did I know that there would be a turning point in all the material value that I was put in the car.

After traveling home from class one evening, I had my radio up high and the amplifiers blowing while my trunk rattled as if there were some dogs playing Frisbee in the inside of it. I was running low on gas and needed to get back home, but I realized that I didn't have my bank card and stopped by my brother's place to borrow a few dollars to make it home.

After leaving there, I traveled west bound towards the interstate to go home. I was working the night shift; it was 8:32 p.m. and shift started at 10 p.m. sharp, as it did every night. I was traveling around 40mph in a neighborhood zone, wanting to quickly get home, change my clothes, eat, and prepare for the full night of work. I felt a slamming sensation and my car was run off the road. It tumbled and almost tipped over. I had been hit from the passenger side, by what I thought was a truck.

I learned later the other car was just as small as mine, but my speed made the impact worse. I held on to the steering wheel as my body was tossed around the car, left to right, with my head hitting the roof, All I could see was my life flashing before me. It felt as if the hit would last forever. I finally had one more slam into the side of a vacant house.

I sat there for a minute, and rubbed for my cheek with my hand to see if I was bleeding. I had no clue where my glasses were, and I could hear my phone vibrating, but did not see where it landed. My leg was throbbing and I was unable to push the driver's door open. I climbed over the passenger side of the vehicle to get out. I was rushing because I thought that the person in the vehicle behind me was dead. I could hear the transformers popping and the tall light pole falling to the ground, and the neighbors in the community came outside. They were in a deep uproar cursing, and yelling "What the hell happened?" People swarmed from all over the street asking were we okay and what happened.

I only remember going northbound to get home, and realized that I didn't have a stop sign, so I must have been blindsided. Fire trucks and EMTs showed up to cut the individual out of the car.

I called my aunt and uncle to explain what was going on, they panicked and rushed to the scene. To realize my first car bought, with so much love and hard work, was lost to a driver that wasn't paying attention shattered my heart. I began to cry wet tears as I walked around my vehicle looking at the damage. Not once did I thank God for my life, or even check on the other person. As people we become so convinced of the value of things, we forget the value of life. God has a way of getting your attention.

The police looked through my car and did a search as they questioned me about what happened. Everything in the car had been thrown around; some of my belongings had been shifted out of the backseat and to the ground, due to the window being down. The only thing that didn't move an inch and remained throughout the wreck was my Bible that laid in-between the two speakers on the backseat. I was lost for words, and stunned because I realized that God allowed for me to walk away from that traumatic accident breathing, speaking, and existing. All I had to recover from was a killer headache and a bruised knee.

I valued materialistic things to the point I began to forget who I was. The importance of the cultivating a true image of self, aligned with God's desire for my life, is what I took away from this situation. Life is good, short, and some don't make it, but I did. This was one more hurdle I battled to get through.

Cool Down

They say things get rough in the downhill stretch. This race is really pushing my limit and I think about the moments in life where it wasn't all good, but I made it work for what was necessary. Life will force you to make very hard, but necessary, adjustments. Life circumstances and pressure will have you thinking and adjusting to weird feelings and emotions all the time. When you tell your story and keep it raw, uncut and unapologetic, you have to choose to not care less about who feels or condones your behavior. We all know right from wrong.

Ultimately, understanding your purpose and inner self helps you unapologetically accept yourself, and that's what is more important than anything. We as individuals have to accept who are becoming and how that will turn out long term. One thing that I can recall during this specific life-season of grief was that changes will come, and when they do can we embrace the change, both the good and ugly.

Just Make the right Decision…

This is easier said than done, but we have to gauge the decisions that we are making. Thoughtless decisions will put our life in the best or worst situations quicker than we know.

My first job working at the juvenile detention was eye opening as hell! To had just been incarcerated a few years before in juvenile, getting a job working in that population was a dream for a while. But this was the beautification in the journey. I went from being in the streets, being involved in a gang, hanging around men that were more dangerous than myself to working in juvenile detention. Can you believe this? I had the opportunity to work in a similar place as I was locked up. And I had the option of influencing these young minds. I had a real opportunity to tell these youth that the life you may want to be involved in is not what it is made out to be, and going to college, getting a trade, and hanging around positive folks is really the path you want to be on. GOD had a way of rerouting my journey. I could be the person to help pull these young people through their own fire and say "I was once in their shoes, now I'm here to help them be better." You can do it too.

Starting my job working at the juvenile detention facility was about needing to pay the rent and be productive, but it soon become my sanctuary. I spoke to the youngsters about staying out of trouble, being better with their parents, and listening to the elders—basically the stuff that I didn't do and actually played a huge part of me being incarcerated in the first place.

The foundation knowledge that keeps people free starts inside the home and telling the youth once you become a master at these things you will be able to stay away from being behind bars. realizing that most of our young people obviously are harmed by poverty and systemic issues of why the school-prison pipeline is hopeful, but it takes basic parenting and a foundation built on the long view to stay out of the system. I didn't appreciate the journey at first. I took it in stride that I was able to contribute to the youth detained in there, but later on I realized that I was making a huge difference for those young brothers and sisters.

My advice to you: Take every moment and exchange serious with anyone you come in contact with! I would later bump into young brothers at the local mall or store, and they told me how I changed their life, and they look up to me from since being released in juvenile. GAMETIME: these are the things we want to see, Be the Change and take it seriously. You never know how much you will be the difference in their life or circumstance.

Be Yourself, Don't Try and Keep Up...

Every young black brother in the early 2000's wanted a "Bubble" Chevy. I thought this was the key to my overall success as a young brother. What I never thought about was the impact of trying to mesh my identity with everyone else, and every other black man in his early 20's in the city of Little Rock.

I didn't stop and think about if this was something I really wanted to do or was I only doing this because it was cool. However, you couldn't have told me any different at that time. I would go to work at the juvenile during the day and still the neighborhood guy by night. Going to parties, clubs, and chasing the honeys on the weekends was still my type of daily flow. As long as my youth, or folks at work, didn't find out I was doing good. That's what I was thinking in my head.

To be one person during the day and another outside of work might be typical for some of us, but why that doesn't make it healthy. Where do we draw the line for true authenticity and to live our truths completely regardless of who is around? I felt that I was playing a game with the man in the mirror; I knew that I could be better and didn't have to live a double life.

One thing that we never realize that people will accept us for who we are, as long as we believe and know to be true to who we are. Today, after reading this cool down, you can walk away from any issue of being like anybody else, and live your TRUTH! It will seem weird at first, but this is the way to go, and you will be set FREE! That horrible wreck I had was a wakeup call, and I am glad that I lived through that accident to tell my story to you all today. Not the story of overcoming a horrible accident, but figuring out how to BREAK OUT OF IDENTITY and realize who the man in the mirror really was and ultimately becoming.

Chapter 8
Hitting the Wall

People often come into your life for seasons and reasons. After sustaining that horrible accident, I didn't lose my passion for cars it only grew stronger. I was in search of a tribe who shared my passion for cars. Little Rock was becoming known for car shows, with people coming together to showcase and celebrate upgrades and unique modifications to their cars. This was more popular in the black community, with guys taking an old school Chevrolet or an old police Crown Victoria and putting some glossy paint and big wheels on it.

I had graduated from the Chevrolet club and begun to explore Ford Crown Victoria's. I remember saving my school refund checks to buy my first one, which was a 2006 police model style, with extended shocks in the rear, and a hard engine. Imagine an old police car with the cage still attached, purchased straight from the auction, and put out on the roads. That was me. I was happy because the Crown Victoria's had become a trend with the young black male demographic. It was the new muscle vehicle of the late 2000's.

There were some guys across the river, north of Little Rock, who had a car group. With fewer than ten guys, I was captivated by their sense of unity. They were flashy and untouchable, the dream team. Their cars had loud pipes, glossy paint, rims painted or super shiny, and extensive music systems. I began to follow these brothers with hopes of being part of that unity.

My crown Victoria didn't stand a chance, but I was eager, and I wanted to see what I could do to make this happen, with two pretty good jobs, I could bring my coins together and make it happen. I bought my first set of 22's, which was just the beginning. Then, I purchased new exhaust tips and put a few decals in my window representing the Ford Tough Life.

After riding the rims for a few months, I wasn't getting the attention the guys from across the river were. I was told you must ride 24-inch rims or better to stay in the race and be an up-and-comer.

It was a competitive game; what looked so good on the outside was spending endless cash, and constantly accommodating the structure your car to fit bigger rims and add different perks. I went and traded my 22-inch rims in, and got some 24-inch rims, painted the insert of the rims, painted my car a fresh white coat of paint and upgraded the exhaust tips; I was almost there.

In a matter of months, I was getting a few more looks in traffic, but couldn't outweigh the daily rough ride I was getting going to work and school in my car. It was competitive, so no one helped each other. It was all about who had the best, and how could they achieve something better quickly enough to make your car not the best. I struggled with the idea of how guys came together over a common subject, but invested in cars and not each other.

At this point, I was purely addicted. I finally purchased my first set of 26-inch rims and was the happiest man in town. Those rims changed my life.

After a night at the club with some friends, I was driving home at one in the morning. I dropped my friend off and took a different route home for a change. I was so tired; I remember having the heaviest eyes as I drove back to my aunt's house. It was the usual: drive slowly and turn my music down. Everything I had on my vehicle was a nuisance and the neighbors were mostly long terms couples and families.

As I turned the corner on my street, I noticed a white Crown Victoria with dark tinted windows parked at the curb. I hadn't ever noticed it before, but I was so tired all I could think about was the pillows calling my name.

I pulled into the yard and said a prayer before for the car to not be gone. This was usual for me. It was 4:33 a.m. and I was out.

Later, there was a loud noise and I heard somebody calling, "RoRo!" That was my childhood nickname. My brother was asking if I parked outside or left my car at my friend's house. It had only been a few hours since I lay down.

I paused and said it should be outside.

He replied, "No, it's not. It's GONE."

I jumped out the bed and rushed towards the front door, no t-shirt, barefooted, and heart pounding through my chest. It was indeed gone. I felt like my eyes were playing tricks on me.

I panicked and went back into the house to wake my uncle up and tell him that the car was gone. He jumped out of his bed and rushed to the front yard as well. There was glass broken on the street.

All I could hear was my aunt's voice in my head, "Son you need an alarm system." I had invested so much into my car and I had no protection. I didn't always keep my insurance current. I was just the average irresponsible young brother that would put his shoe on before he attempted to tie them.

My heart was broken and all I could think about was that white car around the corner with the tinted windows. I felt betrayed, used, and angry. Days passed and the police found the car in a neighboring town, damaged, and of course, the rims and speakers gone. Over the next few months the current crew I was with split up. There was a lot of arguing and talks about who was in charge, and slowly everyone went their own way.

I still loved cars and was blessed enough to a meet a guy from Texas who introduced me to Crown Vic Boys (CVB). They were a national movement that brings people together to build each other and their cars up. He and I eventually worked to form a local chapter. The Dream Team was born.

Three months passed, and we had membership of thirty members. As positive as it sounds, things were not quite friendly. We did not vet our members and a lot of them had a lot of questionable social connections. There were thieves, drug dealers, and con artists. If you can name it, they were present. As bad as we fought to launch this movement, we weren't able to screen good candidates and it hurt us in the end. I wanted to create my first car with a flashy paint/wrap job. I had seen some good jobs done, but couldn't afford the price. I saved my money for a few months and came up with a brilliant idea. I wanted to put the wrap of the Facebook Logo on my car. Sounds weird, right? During the early 2000s there was demand for cars with brands and company names on cars. I was scared of some of the attention I would get, but I did it.

This was a two-month process, week after week of designs, phone calls to the company who was making the material, getting custom rims done to match the car, and an extensive system with TVs and explosive speakers. It took about five months to finish. I was amazed that I dared to be so different. I pulled out of the shop sporting big rims, a car wrap with the Facebook logo all over it, and the prettiest navy and light blue colors that represent Facebook from the bottom of the rear to the top of the hood.

The next few hours my phone rang over thirty times, random strangers in traffic stopped me to get pictures, ladies followed me from one stop light to the next to see who was driving, and to have a conversation. I was elated; this was what I wanted. Over the next few months I would receive ample attention from social media, laughing gestures from people who thought it was a ridiculous idea to create such car, and old and new friends who wanted to exploit the fact that they met the man driving the Facebook car.

One evening, coming home, I met this young lady at a gas station. She was very attractive: roughly 5'2," with nice hips, hair that reached her hips, the prettiest smile, and laugh. I pumped gas and I listened to her have a conversation on her phone.

With my heart beating swiftly I was able to utter "Hello." She spoke back, I began to ask her where she was from and did, she has a boyfriend. She said no, but claimed she wasn't interested in getting to know anyone.

I replied, "If you give me the chance, I can make you smile and perhaps you can give me a chance to take you on a date." She paused and said "I will take your number." I wasn't used to a challenge or hesitation.

When we went on our first date; she was emphasized that her mom and dad would not be so hip to my car and image. Be mindful I stood 5"9, was a heavyweight, had gold teeth and a few noticeable tattoos, and drove this flashy car with big rims and a car wrap. I understood. I wasn't a hoodlum for sure, but of course society didn't see it that way. I felt belittled and ashamed. I thought everyone would look past my exterior to see my likes and passions.

She wouldn't let me pull into her driveway and agreed to meet me down the street and would park, elsewhere while we drove to the restaurant. I was fine with that. My heart fluttered as we held conversation, she questioned me about my past, what type of women I dated, and what did I see in her.

It was this weird feeling I got while being with her, it felt so right. Twenty-three-years-old, I had never experienced love from another woman. I couldn't imagine what that looked or felt like. All I knew what infatuation.

Over the next few months we had the best times. We shared beautiful laughs together. She was the first girl I ever stayed overnight with on a consistent basis, we would cook together, travel together, and she seriously supported my car club activities endeavor; this was my type of lady.

Our first road trip we bonded so closely. The distraction of other women never left. From time to time I would entertain the frequent Facebook messages, and even held a few conversations from time to time with other women. I wouldn't commit to sex with them, and that's how I knew that I really liked her. Any other woman I had dealt with I would cheat around, especially in my younger days. I had no standard and didn't really understand the importance of loyalty and commitment in a relationship with man and woman. While trying to keep up with the Joneses in the streets, I was trying to commit to a relationship with this beautiful young lady. From time to time I would struggle with how to please her; this was an issue for me.

I never had a man sit me down and explain how to treat a woman. True enough, I had older siblings and cousins who would drop nuggets, but as a young man it's vital that this information is transparent. We would have disagreements, a few heated arguments but nothing to crazy, but sometimes they wouldn't end the right way.

One disagreement ended horribly with the words "I hate you" being said by both of us. We were young and had crazy emotions about each other, but didn't know the true commitment of keeping each other happy. We struggled to balance time for each other with wanting to live as unattached young adults. We would sometimes go a week without speaking to each other, but deep down wanting and craving attention. She was the first girl that to bring me to tears because of the sincerity and care she gave me. Despite my deep affection for her, I struggled with treating her badly and having a bad word with her. By not having my biological parents raise me as a couple and see model stable, healthy affection to was tough. We soon come to an end and broke up.

The largest car show in the state was held annually and I always attended, just to show off my new additions from the previous year. It was a big festival where all car gurus would come together for an all-day event, to network and showoff their rides. That year, when was asked to put my car in the show for the "Best Ride of The Year," I hesitated. I felt that the competition was too upscale for my car. My buddies really pushed me and I decided to put my car in the show.

When it was time for the prizes, they announced the awards starting with 3rd place and ending with the winner. The room got quiet and there were three of us still standing after the first two were crowned. The other owners also had nervous looks on their face, reflecting the uncertainty of what the host would announce next. "And the 1st place award of the "Grand Car show of Arkansas goes to: The Facebook car!"

My heart was filled with joy; I was intensely excited, and couldn't believe I had won the show! My dreams had come true, after five long years of dedication and work I had made it to the #1 spot. I got into cars because I had a real passion and it leaked to wanting to be the best and most creative. The trophy was so huge. There was excitement from the crew that came with me from home. We traveled a few hours to come have a good time and left with trophies.

Not too long after my win, I had gotten off work late on a Friday night and decided to go home and rest up for the weekend. But I got a call from a close friend to meet up and share a conversation before he traveled out the country for a few weeks. I value friendship and loyalty. I left the house near midnight and my aunt asked me, "Son, you sure you going to leave? You tired. It's late. You should stay in." I replied, "It won't be long. I will be back shortly."

I cruised down the street at 45 mph with my music up high. As I crossed an intersection, from out of nowhere, a car with bright head lights smashed into the front of my car. In the back of my mind, in the middle of this collision, the wreck that happened a few years before was playing back. This time, the other car ran into a pole and nearly flipped over. I was breathless, and my body had flown across the other seat during the hit. I could barely move. In my mind it felt like Deja vu. In my mind I kept telling myself no way, this is a dream, I can't be in another accident. It was no dream. I was part of a massive accident that involved four vehicles. I climbed to the other seat to open the door, and I could hear screaming and people yelling for help. The vehicle in the next lane had caught fire from the collision.

I panicked. I couldn't believe what was happening. It was totally shocking to be part of another tragic accident, but yet again I was saved by my Lord, Jesus Christ. I was breathing and even though my vision was blurry due to my glasses being thrown from my face, I was okay.

The paramedics and ambulances made it to the scene to help and take reports. As I sat there and reminisced about the hard work and value that I put into my car, I evaluated all that happened to me. My car was gone; it was shattered to pieces and it was tilted over from its super extended shocks that held up the big rims. I thought, this door is closing and new doors will open. I had been into custom cars for five years and had invested thousands of dollars into creative cars and custom fixings for them. I had suffered two bad wrecks and a stolen vehicle, but won a first-place trophy from the largest show in the state.

My heart was at ease as I rode in the back of the ambulance. My anger was slowly going away. I was glad to be living and breathing, the police officer said he was glad no one died. We all reach points in life where the door shuts, and we, as people, cannot pull on that door open again. At that moment, I understood the heartaches, the successes, and even the midpoints of this five-year journey that took my life in another direction.

Cool Down

Your race is speeding up, others besides you are beginning to pass you (and quickly, I must add). Will I come in first? Will my time be right? Will those who have been cheering me on be on the right page? All these different things going through my head are beginning to cross over. Often in life we get distracted by what other people around us are doing, and usually we get sidetracked from the goal we set. We are getting tired and weary; I can remember during the time of finding a car tribe (clique) and feeling that I needed the community and network of brothers around me to help fuel the fire that was inside of me. The truth behind this is I didn't necessarily need that tribe, maybe a few of the people who support you and believe in you will suffice, but not a large group of people.

As I stated in the previous chapters, to meet our goals we have the right amount of support behind us. The race is ours, and if we slow up some that doesn't mean that we won't come in, we'll still finish and meet our own goals and ambitions. By hitting a wall, we realize that we need some more support because life is stretching us thin, and we are losing our wind. But we can't give up on what we initially started. The time is to refuel, refocus, and press through the mark. The finish line is near!

Lead with with a Clear Heart and Intention…

I can remember getting involved in the Car Club (the Crown Vic Boys) and all the excitement it brought. I was ecstatic as hell to be a part of this illustrious club that already had a solid and winning reputation. One thing that I missed out on earlier during this process was that I was called to lead, one thing about being in leadership and being asked to be a part of something is doubting our desire before we're given the chance to get started. We begin to mentally strip ourselves of our potential and intent.

But why do we question how good we will do in a certain position or group of people if we know that our heart and intention is in the right place. Honestly, once you set your heart to lead righteously things will begin to come about, and you don't have to be concerned about the outside forces. Good energy and intention always overcome any situation.

When I was led to lead the Crown Vic Boys (CVB), I didn't think I had any prior experience in leadership. But I had unique life experiences (ULE's). These are different times throughout our lives where we have undergone tremendous changes and struggles and figured out a way to overcome these obstacles, or have a unique way of how we dealt with the circumstance. So, your Unique Life Experiences gives you the credibility to lead.

I hit the wall several times during my journey of fooling with that car stuff; I went from putting a lot of money and time in to this journey, got a car stolen, and my privacy was invaded by the thieves who took my valuable asset, plus there was trust issues that were developed. Through all of this I was still able to lead those guys that were a part of the club with me. I didn't know who actually stole the car and if someone set me up to be the one to go through the loss or not. What I realized being in this club and being the leader was I still needed to lead with a clear heart and intention.

Remember during your journey of betrayal or difficulty to still lead with a clear heart and intention. You are the Master of your Destiny, the Captain of your Soul!

Push Pass the Pain the Win will Come…

After all the mess you have gone through, no wonder you are ready to call it quits. But you can't—it's just not a part of the plan, and you are stronger than what you think. I can remember going through all the heartaches with that vehicle stuff, having to stay up to social standards with the world, and it was getting difficult to deal with. I wondered: Will times become normal again? Can I just get a break?

The thoughts running inside my head were draining. As I was getting burned out on the street life and trying to maintain my image, I encouraged myself by saying the pain will have to end at some point. The dysfunctional relationships, negative interactions with people close to me, and lack of trust was equating to me making my way out of the street life, car-game, and winning a first-place trophy.

For five years I dedicated my life to just keeping up with the Joneses and staying relevant, but the time was over and my time was fruitful for sure. That trophy symbolizes more than a shiny gloss paint job and big rims. Its exemplified perseverance, a strong heart, and someone who didn't give up. All the money, late nights, and maintenance didn't matter once I came in first place for Best Car in the State. We have to think about the difficulties troubling us on our journey, or in daily life, and realize that soon you will get your first-place trophy. Time will seem long and, yes, you will become impatient, but just remember your goal and what you started your path to success for in the first place.

Your trophy is waiting; don't give up, YOU'RE ALMOST THERE!

Chapter 9
Breaking Stride

Often times we think about using the power of momentum to have breakthroughs or get results. Sometimes to keep going, you don't need momentum, you need to break stride. When I think about how much I learned as a young adult, I often wonder how could I continue to gain momentum to break into the next stage of happiness and quality of life.

I spent more time in undergraduate than the average working college student, because of majority of my effort went into seeking popularity, increasing my social circles, and getting involved in the car life. I would often get down on myself, or feel inadequate, when I realized that I was going on my sixth semester of my bachelor's degree. I was seeing a lot of my high school and college friends continue moving forward, getting good jobs, get married, and even have children.

The delays and losses made me a better man. The heart of becoming a better person, with a testimony to share is helping those who didn't have hope get through their mess. I went through a lot of disarray, but your mess, just like my mess, is your story, and your story can change the world and inspire others to change their mindset. We have the power in our stories to influence change.

At twenty-four I was taking a heavy hour load in school and working two jobs rewarding, but stressful jobs. I was making good money, with great benefits, and had the opportunity to impact others. I felt like I was living out my true calling.

The prior semester I had a talk with my academic advisor who informed me I would soon run out of government financial assistance for school. I didn't have the best grades and lost every scholarship that was given for not fulfilling the requirements of the scholarship. The only way I could get through college was to take out student loans. But I had set my goals and was not turning back after already facing such adversity. I was determined to finish. I owed it to my family and my community and myself.

I realized that God allowed a young black man with much that had been lost to still reach the marker of success. I was sure that my natural parents, if they had still been alive, would want me to keep pushing. I had been to juvenile at seventeen years old for not being a leader and getting caught up in being a follower. I had been whopped emotionally by my third-grade teacher for telling me I wouldn't amount to anything and having me tested for ADHD as a way to get me out of her class and into special education classes. I spent time away from home as an eight-year-old because of grief that led to behavior issues.

All of this is my story. You must love your good, bad, and ugly of your story. Breaking stride will drive you to the finish line.

The phone rang and I heard a voice of a woman. I had seen her in the last few months, but we weren't currently together. She started to remind me of who she was, but I couldn't match her voice with a memory. She went on to explain that we met, and hung out a few times, and even reminded me of the Facebook Car. She told me that she was a few months pregnant and we needed to talk face-to-face, this was not what I expected to hear from an anonymous number.

I began to stutter and ask if she had reached the right person. She was positive. We had slept together and she recently found out she was pregnant. I was the only guy she had slept with.

She said again we needed to talk more and face-to-face.

All I could think about was what this meant for me. I was nervous about what my aunt and uncle would think. I didn't want to think about how people around me would feel. When I imagined having kids, I imagined that I would be this old man and situated financially with a good job.

I began to deny responsibility and demanded a blood test, and challenged her to take me to court. I made my mind up and this couldn't happen to me. Indeed, I convinced myself it could not be true. I had never cared for anyone but myself; I never even had a younger sibling to look after. I was simply selfish and inconsiderate in my dealings with others, and the reality and responsibility of having a child scared me. The truth is, she was correct. We did engage sexually.

The next two months were stressful. I was getting though my last semester of school and working two jobs. Being an adult and paying the bills wasn't as pretty as I imagined. I continued to tell my aunt and other family members the same story I told myself, it was not possible I was the father. They were convinced. But creating a child is a possibility for anyone who is sexually active.

I didn't know she was my daughter yet, but my baby girl was born on July 29, 2012. Leading up to her birth I had prayed and asked for discernment about if I was the father and peace for whatever the truth was. I prayed to be the best father I could be if she was mine. I knew the parent figures provided by my aunt and uncle taking me in was the best thing that could have happened to me and I was committed to be that for my own child.

One evening I came home from work, and there was an envelope with The Office of Child Support Enforcement as the return address. My anxiety was high as I ripped off the edges of the tall white envelope. My short stubby hands reached in the package to pull the papers out. I was sweating bullets as my eyes scanned the words on the canary yellow paper and my pupils felt as if they were burning like a house fire.

"You are 99.9 percent the father." I couldn't breathe for about twenty seconds. I immediately knew it was time to step up and be the man I was called to be. Accountability was on the horizon and being deadbeat was not on my agenda. I never had the chance to spend time with my father or my biological mother. I felt the urge to fill a space that wasn't filled for me as a young person.

The first time I saw my daughter changed my life. My heart felt like a bucket of gold and my tears ran like the Mississippi River. It was love at first sight; the call to action of being a man, and working through the calling of fatherhood was precious to me.

In my last semester it seemed like I got no rest, but I was determined to finish the race of school. The last month of school was approaching and my mind was all over the place. I was a new father, my work life was busy, and the workload of school was as heavy as a ton of bricks.

One of my favorite instructors, Mr. Davis, motivated me by telling me that God gives his heavy loads and sharp assignments to those who can bear them and execute well in his vision. To make such a paradigm shift I had to understand that I was chosen and made with a purpose that was for more than me.

When I finished college, I was the first generation in my family to walk across the stage. My walk was for all the brothers that didn't make it, those incarcerated that wished they could have made it, and for the black men and women who don't feel they are smart enough to finish school. In conquering the journey of my college education, I leave a legacy for others, my newly born child, and myself. We have the power to shift the channels and set others up for success.

I received notification that the semester was complete and that I would graduate college with my Bachelors of Arts in Human Services in May of 2015. My emotions rang deep and all I could feel was the load being lifted. After almost seven years of being in college it would soon come to a beautiful finish.

In the last 400 meters of a track race, runners pick up the speed and break their stride to reach the last leg of the race. I was a changed man and I knew who Jesus was. I realized that I had support and that was all I needed. I had acquired a college degree when I was supposed to be in prison or dead from a deep-rooted street life. I accepted the new quest of continuing to develop and be the best man I could be, to all mankind and myself.

My mother and father would be proud. I can still picture them smiling and rooting me on as I push strong to be the winner of my race. You own your race. Never give up on your journey. Keep pushing! See it through!

Cool Down

Life transitions are always interesting. As humans we are supposed to evolve, we are not supposed to be the same as we started off. This means we have to be mindful that with time comes growth, and with growth comes new opportunity and responsibility.

I think back on that call I got during my early, young adult life when I found out that I would be a father. It was the best thing that has happened to me. My daughter truly helped me to cap the fact that as time evolves you will become someone different, with a new identity, sense of understanding, and seriousness about life itself.

I am not endorsing children before marriage, nor am I endorsing that you should be having sex before marriage. What I am saying is that regardless of the decisions you come to, remember there is beauty even in the hard parts. There are disadvantages to not being married and having children. Co-parenting from miles away can be difficult, but there is beauty in being a responsible father and leading your child to be great in ways that you couldn't and providing a good blueprint to life.

Having support players such as Mr. Davis is sometimes what we all need during the most difficult, but rewarding moments—that one person you may be blowing off while you just had to settle with news or new life experiences may be the best person to help lead you toward your vision, responsibility, and success. Honestly, as a new father I couldn't imagine not having anyone to talk to about my experiences. You don't know how to adapt to their mother once you all are not together anymore, how to not say the wrong thing, and better yet how to not create this toxic bond between you both that will ultimately affect the child long term. There's a head full of thoughts, but the support of a good friend and trusted advisor will help you to see things will be fruitful during these moments.

When you have been battling with an illness, it's sometimes hard to be happy and positive because we realize are the energy that we wish to get back. I think back on all the times during my educational journey of how I always came in last, held back with poor grades, etc. Every single thing about being a young black man in the educational system gave me every reason to not want to pursue it. I made the choice to work hard, despite the pressure against me.

After achieving my undergraduate degree at a four-year college, I couldn't believe that I had made it that far. I worked hard and did my due diligence to get to that place, but I had every reason to quit. We can't quit once our divine success is on the other side. Next time you face a really difficult moment or triumph, get in your quiet place, close your eyes, and visualize you overcoming that thing that went against you. While you are meditating on this success, repeat slowly. I AM, I WILL, I HAVE Overcome. I will WIN, I HAVE WON ALREADY!

Chapter 10
I Made It Through

When I think of racing and endurance, I think of track athletes that run relays. They don't run alone and each person's race matters. It takes the entire relay team finishing their leg of the race for the anchor to take over and finish the last leg. The anchor spends the whole race waiting and visualizing the end. Like an anchor, you have to know your true calling and what destiny has laid out for you.

My life seemed to come full circle when right before graduation I received a phone call from a professor that was more like a mentor. She motivated me, gave me a chance as an undergraduate, and actually believed in me. She had a question: "Would I be interested in speaking at my college commencement?" I was in a deep shock and didn't know how to answer. My initial answer was no, but after a week of praying and practicing speaking, I called her to tell her yes. My family was blown away and supported the decision. I had been waiting on this moment my entire life. I kept running the race.

My race didn't end there. Since that graduation I completed a master's degree and went on to work for the Arkansas Department of Human Services as a Medicaid caseworker. I left my job in July of 2017 to take a risk and become a full-time entrepreneur. I knew that I loved to serve others and my history in mental health and working with families was priceless.

I planted a vision to become a community contributor/activist and founded a nonprofit organization. I, like many others, could not ignore the call to create social change. And those who have lived through those issues and come out on the other side are charged to take the on role of helping those who can't help themselves.

I devoted nearly a decade of my life in the system to helping others hurt by poverty, economic issues, or a broken criminal justice system. My new endeavor is outside the system.

I founded The Confess Project. It targets young men of color, in local and global communities, with mental health education, through inspiring hope and healthy dialogue. This project allows me to share my own struggles, but also give tangible ways and solutions for others working through similar trials. I help young men who look just like me through mentoring.

Our lives are not supposed to be ordinary because the race of life was not designed to be ordinary. We must navigate the curves of life, blast through hurdles, and stride to cross the finish line.

I'm a work in progress, and the race of life has been both fast and weary, but I have persevered and I am still running the race of life.

About the Author

Lorenzo P. Lewis is a social entrepreneur, professional speaker, and founder of the widely acclaimed The Confess Project, an initiative that centers on mental health and wellness for young men of color.

A master storyteller, Lewis has spoken at numerous venues around the country about his journey turning pain into purpose—from narrowly escaping the school-to-prison pipeline and obtaining a master's degree to his current work building a national mental health movement.

He lives in Little Rock, Arkansas.